Heavy Call,

Lonely Walk

by

DaRain

Dominion Life Ministries, Inc.™

7417 Canaveral Rd. Jacksonville, FL

First published by AuthorHouse 2/14/2008

Second Edition by Dominion Life Ministries, Inc. 07/29/2015

ISBN: 978-0-578-01206-3 (sc)

Printed in the United States of America

This book is printed on acid-free paper.

Contents

The Most Holy Place

Acknowledgements

I would like to express my deepest gratitude to the following:

THE MOST HOLY PLACE

My Heavenly Father – You are so true and good, my Abba Father. We're not done, Daddy!

My King and Savior, Jesus Christ – I am crucified with you Lord…All the ends of the earth are coming to you. Thank you for entrusting me with your ministry and this Heavy Call. Speak Lord.

My Comforter, The Holy Spirit – Although the walk has been lonely, you have never left me alone. Thank you, Holy Spirit. I need your presence every second of every day.

THE INNER COURT

My wife- Sharon D. Powell… You are my prophecy fulfilled… I am in Him, with You.

Pastor Alvin R. and Apostle Brenda Ashley – Thank you for birthing me into the ministry, and giving me tough love. I will never forget your contribution to my life.

To my birth children – Ericka, D.J., Phillip, Trinity – you are my pride and joy.

My Mother, Barry Jones – The man I am is because of you. You are the most virtuous woman I know.

And in loving memory of the following – Mary Ada Brown, James L. Brown, Jr., Rev. James "The Preacher" Brown (Savannah), Pastor George E. Hilton (Church of the Firstborn) and my stepfather Wayne L. "Bulldog" Powell (he did the best he could with what he had).

THE OUTER COURT

My brother Pastor Wayne J. Greenfield and family, Jada, Jazzy, Joshua, Dana, members of Christ Center Church in Shreveport (now that's faith), Zerick "Playwriter" Jones and wife, Cedarian Crawford and wife Jenena, the cast of "Sanctified Theft", "I Need My Spouse Back, and "If Your Dirty Take A Bath" , my mentor Tim Storey and the late Dr. Myles Munroe, the members of Dominion Life Ministries, Aunt Aris (everyone needs an aunt like you), the greatest couple I've ever known uncle Wayne and the late Ann Tribbett, Lorie and family (holy hooah!), #Team Healthy, and my sisters Deanna,Birdie, Jersella, Maryellen, Nancy, Angie, Michelle, Brittany and Jakira (never forget).

Foreword

I remember when Pastor Powell walked into my church several years ago. It was a pivotal time in my ministry, as I endeavored to walk out and pioneer the "heavy call" on my life to rise up an army of fortified believers who would know the will of God, the ways of God and the wisdom of God by His word.

As this book suggests, becoming subjugated by the whisper, the small still voice of the Holy Spirit, to embrace destiny is not something to be taken lightly! Accepting "the call" can leave you suspended, breathless, as you witness the power of God while simultaneously, it may appear dreadful when we realize our weaknesses, insufficiencies and shortcomings apart from the indwelling of the Father!

Through the principles of faith, obedience, submission, love and leading of the Holy Spirit we can answer this clarion call with boldness and confidence! I am pleased that there are individuals like Minister Powell, who have expressed his heartfelt compassion to help others in the "household of faith" through penmanship.

I pray that the pages of this book will inspire many to embrace the principles of the Holy Scriptures and know that the gifts and calling of God are irrevocable and without repentance, with God all things are possible! "For verily I say unto you, that whosoever shall say unto this mountain, be thou removed, and be thou cast into the sea; and shall not doubt in his heart, but shall believe that those things which he saith shall come to pass; he shall have whatsoever he saith." (Mark 11:23)

- Pastor Alvin Ashley (Christ Center Church)

Dedication

I dedicate this book to my grandfather, the late James L. Brown, Sr. My grandfather was hardest working man I've ever met. A former soldier in the Army during the Korean War, he was also a civil service employee at Dover Air Force Base in Dover, Delaware for 30+ years. I never met anyone who endured grief so gracefully or tragedy so triumphantly. I love you, Dad.

INTRODUCTION

An Objective Intrinsic Look at Me (this means you!)

1 Corinthians 11:28 "But let a man examine himself, and so let him eat of that bread, drink of that cup."

I trust that the pages contained within the covers of this book are enriching for your personal edification. Make no mistake about it; you have a heavy call on your life. Even if you have never answered God's call for your life, or have been misaligned in the wrong call, God's perfect will is for you to spend quality time with Him in a lonely place. I know this message is from the heart of God to your heart, but your submitted, willing and open heart is needed to fully grasp the urgency of what God wants to convey to you. So are you ready to answer your heavy call? Now when you respond to the call, do you understand that at times it may very well be a lonely walk? It's time for an honest, self-examination of your status with God. As we perform a synoptic overview of Heavy Call, Lonely Walk, pray about making the necessary changes for your life.

Chapter 1

You must settle within yourself you have been called by God to a holy vocation. You must understand that this call is a mandate, not a suggestion and God wants to spend time with you to fully develop your call. Motivation is a key part of your success, but you can't be motivated to fulfil your call if you don't know what your call is. You may feel lonely during this process, but you are not alone. God is strengthening you to be all you can be for Him.

Chapter 2

There are various types of calls in God's Kingdom. God wants very much for all of us to answer the particular call He is issuing. Most believers want to answer God's call but haven't recognized which type of call to answer. Either God will confirm the call Himself or He will place a spiritually responsible person in your path to assist in your call development.

Chapter 3

As you are developing in your call, you may feel an overwhelming sense of loneliness. You are not alone, God is with you, and decisions you make regarding your life will come from a renewed relationship with Christ. The more you spend time with God, the more you will see how excellent you are.

Chapter 4

God has called you to a lonely place to deal with your body, soul and spirit. The place in which He deals with your body is called the habitation of initial surrender. There are different types of wilderness experiences, just as there are different types of calls. God wants to give you true revelation about who He is and who you are while you're in the wilderness.

Chapter 5

If you are ever to fulfill your call, then you must rid yourself of distractions which cause you to lose your tunnel vision. There are many examples of leaders who have had to walk alone or chose to walk alone to fulfill the call on their life. There are biblical, as well as modern day examples of this type of leadership.

Chapter 6

The second surrender God requires from you is the surrender of your soul. God will bring you to a lonely place so that you can master the soulish part of your life. Everyone is not equipped to endure your Garden of Gethsemane experience with you.

Chapter 7

There is a distinct difference between counsel and opinion. Both can be deterrents to you fulfilling the call on your life. You must walk in your kingdom authority and discern the usefulness of people's opinions and counsel in your life.

ix

Chapter 8

There are times when life will hit you hard and you will find yourself all alone. It's okay for you to question God regarding the pain you are going through. No one knows the pain you are going through except you and your Heavenly Father. God's perfect will for you is that you obtain the victory needed to bring you eternal victory in Him.

Chapter 9

The institution of marriage is in disarray. Half of marriages end up in divorce and God is not pleased. The understanding of why marriages fail lies in two individuals discovering their true identity in Christ. If you are single and preparing to marry, or married and feel unfulfilled in your marriage, this chapter must become embedded as a personal part of your self-examination.

Chapter 10

The final surrender for your life is often the most neglected. It is the surrender of your deepest spiritual wounds to the healing power of Christ that will catapult you into the best years of your life. Even though darkness may surround you, it's after this time of commending the broken areas of your spirit to God that you will experience the glory of Almighty God in your life.

This book accomplishes a two-fold purpose for you as you read. First, it will help define exactly what a divine call is. You must understand that whenever you have a heavy call on your life, God will call you to a lonely place. Why would God call you to a lonely place? The answer to this question is made clear in the second purpose of this book. It is necessary from God's perspective to do so in order that you know yourself, get better acquainted with the call on your life, and the God in your life. May God bless you in your growth as he guides you through your heavy call.... your lonely walk

Chapter 1

Why Do I Have to Be Alone?

"I'm in the Army in the now!" I gleamed to my uncle J.R. as we conversed on the phone. J.R. was more than an uncle, he was like my older brother as he was only four years my senior. "I'm getting out of Delaware for a while. I joined the National Guard. I've got to go Oklahoma for training" My life had brought me to this point. My poor decisions had brought to this point. I needed a change. "You sure about this?" J.R.'s question in itself was a subvert indictment of doubt in my sudden choice. To this point in my life, it seemed like everything in my life was a failure. "Yeah, I'm sure." But I wasn't really sure. If I had failed so much to this point life, how in the world could I possibly make it in America's army, with tenacious, trained drill sergeants waiting to weed out the weak "Well..."J.R. stated stoically, "All I can say is...take God with you" Little did J.R. or I know that God was already there waiting to direct me to my real call of duty via a detour to a lonely place called Fort Sill Oklahoma.

Why Do I Have To Be Alone?

This perhaps the most difficult literature I have ever written...

The difficulty for me was in acquainting myself with the process of becoming the man, pastor, father, friend and child God desires me to be. The process was not easy for me and it will not be a cake walk for you either. Most of you who engage and embrace the tenets of these pages will have an equal level of discomfort, especially those who can relate to some of the same shared experiences. I want you to allow for three basic understandings. First, you have been called by God. We will deal with the call of God in the second chapter. Second, it is vital that you know and comprehend that this "call" is a mandate from God. Finally, I need you to grasp that if you are truly a believer in Christ you will become motivated by God to become one with Him (body, soul and spirit). The surrender of one's self to God is not natural or normal, but it is necessary. That is – it's necessary if you truly want to be fulfilled in your life. Everyone doesn't want to be fulfilled in life and, make no mistake, everyone won't be.

The Mandate of God

There is certainly a powerful renaissance occurring in the Body of Christ today. Everywhere you turn, someone has graduated to a position, aspired to a title, (you know, Bishop This, Apostle That and so on) or initiated a new church. All seem to have an emphatic revelation or a distinct "word" from God. This is not an indictment against those who have been truly appointed by God to be such. Certainly, it is God's will for the church to grow, and it is God's heart that all men come to the knowledge of His saving grace. I don't know about you, but sometimes I wonder how many of these ministries have been truly mandated by God to perform the services they are engaging in!

A mandate is "to order or commit to someone's charge" or even more literally "give into one's hand". It would be naïve for you and I to believe that everyone who says, "I am this" or "God called me to that" really understand the concept of a mandate from God. A mandate is more than a simple or welcoming plea. It is an actual demand that requires both attention and response.

For example, if you were seriously injured in an automobile accident it wouldn't be enough for you to call the local 911 emergency center, would it? You would require the operator on the other end of the line to pay careful attention to your call. The operator needs to spend enough time with you one the phone to understand the details of your call. You also wouldn't want the operator to be distracted because your health would depend on the accuracy of the information that the operator is recording and relaying to the emergency team. Finally, the 911 operator needs to insure that an adequate and immediate response occurs. If the 911 operator responds to your health crisis by sending a law enforcement officer to a robbery scene, then the response would be inadequate to your need. If the response takes too long the possibility of serious injury (or worse) could happen!

The Body of Christ is the 911 operator God has commissioned to respond to the end-time condition of the world today. However, too often we as believers have

a)   Not paid attention to God's call

b)   Not taken enough time to understand the details of God's call

c)   Responded inadequately

d)   Delayed our response to the call of God.

God's call doesn't fade away. If you choose simply to ignore it, it will only become more resounding. Most people also don't spend enough time with God to understand the details of what God is calling them to do. You see, it's because of the lack of quality time spent with God that many respond inadequately to the call of God. You have to be alone with God in order to know God. They simply get a whiff of God and take off before getting the whole story. There are many who are in the Body of Christ today serving in areas to which God hasn't called them. My prayer is that instead of pridefully maintaining a position in which they haven't been ordained to serve, those persons would conduct a serious self-evaluation and discover their true identity in Christ. Being alone with God also serves another purpose. Many of you don't have the confidence to step out into your true call, and therefore delay (sometimes permanently) God's plan to use your gifts and talents to benefit His church.

God's Might, Your Motivation

Do you remember the most trying time in your life? For some of you it may be the death of a loved one. Others of you may have suffered from a serious health setback. Still others have had to withstand overwhelming financial challenges. Perhaps some of you are still going through these difficulties as you are reading this book. Then again, you may be someone who can eagerly and retrospectively declare that you have overcome some serious trials. For those of you who have survived the trials, do you remember the inner strength that you possessed to make it through your situation?

"Motivated, Motivated/ Downright Motivated...You check us out, you check us out, you, you, you, you, check us out!"

How I remember those early days in the Army when, as a 29 year old recruit, I would bellow this chant in concert with my other platoon "battle buddies". I have to admit that early in my career I wasn't always the most responsive of recruits. My unresponsiveness would often draw the fi re of a drill sergeant who would proceed to discipline me for drawing an unnecessary "heat round" (unwarranted attention). Every recruit went through this process and, after receiving countless repetitions of physical discipline, we as a platoon became a cohesive body of uniformed soldiers.

-Getting "smoked" by a drill sergeant

The motivation required to become cohesive was two-fold. It was first the drill sergeants, who at their discretion deemed it necessary to physically remind of us that anything less than obtaining the Army's standard of performance would result in implementation of their "motivating" technique. Secondly, there was an inner drive that, when ignited, lit a fire under each recruit to achieve higher standards of performance.

This two-fold motivation also operates in the Kingdom of God. First, God puts us in a place, situation or circumstance to bring out the best in us. We, as believers, are not always motivated to do our best. God, as He deems necessary, will implement corrective measures in our respective lives in order to renew our focus on the call He has committed to us. The difference between those who have achieved great accomplishments and those who have not is that many lack the ignition of their inner motivation, which is an individual's major determinant in achievement.

I, like thousands of others in our country, have suffered through the agony of homelessness. The anguish of not having a home to return to was enough motivation for me to move quickly to change my circumstances. Surprisingly though, I learned that everyone doesn't possess the same motivation to remove themselves from peril. In fact, the environment I considered perilous was regarded as comfortable by others who were homeless with me. A year after ending homelessness, many of the same people I befriended were still homeless...by choice!

Don't be fooled. Everyone does not or will not have the same motivation that you have. That's why completion of your heavy call is determined by your lonely walk, as well as the amount of time that you spend with God.

Paul in the Desert

Throughout the scriptures, we are given definitive explanations as to why it is necessary to be alone with God. As believers, we have to usher ourselves into a solitary existence with God. Galatians 1:11-17 given by Apostle Paul gives us a portrait of his conversion experience and subsequent self-exile to Arabia:

"I want you to know, brothers that the gospel I preached is not something that man made up. I did not receive it from any man, nor was I taught it; rather, I received it by revelation from Jesus Christ. For you have heard of my previous way of life in Judaism, how intensely I persecuted the church of God and tried to destroy it. I was advancing in Judaism beyond many Jews of my own age and was extremely zealous for the traditions of my fathers. But when God, who set me apart from birth and called me by his grace, was pleased to reveal his Son in me so that I might preach him among the Gentiles, I did not consult any man, nor did I go up to Jerusalem to see those who were apostles before I was, but I went immediately into Arabia and later returned to Damascus."

These passages allow us to understand several important concepts as to why it's necessary to spend time with God alone.

1.   The Gospel Paul preached was genuine, not a man-made fabrication.

2.   It was received by revelation.

3.   Paul never denied his past.

4.   Paul understood his call was ordained by God himself.

5.   It's not necessary to ask for opinions about your call.

As a believer in Christ, I believe it's not always in the best interest of the church to be hypercritical of other ministries. Generally, I believe that overly criticizing someone who has differing views will only serve to undermine unity in the body. Let's face it; a great deal of preaching is not by revelation, but by man-made fabrication. To reveal something is to "disclose something that was unknown or secret", or "to make something known by divine or supernatural means". True revelation is apparent because this type of revelation should be absent of personal conclusion. Paul never denied that he was a zealous abuser and accuser of the church.

In order for your life to be effectively used for what God wants to do, you have to come to grips with what you have done. When you understand your past, this knowledge clarifies the call of God on your life. You further understand that because God called you individually, you can respond to your call individually and eliminate the need for man's opinion. (See chapter 7)

The Purging Process

John 15:1-2

"I am the true vine, and my Father is the gardener. He cuts off every branch in me that bears no fruit, while every branch that does bear fruit he prunes so that it will be even more fruitful."

Another reason for you to be alone is the fact that Jesus desires that you yield more fruit for the Kingdom. It is vital that God removes items, people, weight, sins, circumstances, trials and tribulations from you in order to heighten your discipline for your call. I'm often intrigued by Christians who feel as though they have "arrived" at a pinnacle of spiritual completion in their life. I'm also astounded at the volume of persons who, once they have achieved a certain plateau in their life, forget about God or loved ones who assisted them in obtaining that plateau.

I believe it is my duty and obligation as an end-time messenger to remind the Body of Christ that we have not "arrived." A litany of reasons why we haven't arrived isn't necessary. Simply ponder on the current state of the church and let that be your reason. As a corporate Body, and as individuals, we in the Body of Christ must continue to bear fruit. Jesus explains that it is necessary to go through a process of purging if you are a believer in Him. There is little difficulty in understanding what type of "fruit" a Christian ought to produce.

Understanding the process which produces the fruit is another matter altogether, though. Fruits are simply those Christ-like attributes that we as Christians should all exhibit. These attributes are outlined for the believer in the fifth chapter of Galatians. The purging process, which is described in John 15:1, is a lifelong process which every believer must go through. Jesus himself went through this process. I define the purging process as the lifelong development of divine character through the removal of carnality and self-will. Every Christian should be like Jesus. 1 Peter 4:1 declares, "Forasmuch then as Christ hath suffered for us in the flesh, arm yourselves likewise with the same mind..."

Jesus deliberately and knowingly underwent this lifelong purging process in order to fulfill the mission from the Father. The purging process can be separated into the three areas of your existence. Those areas are your body, soul and spirit.

1.   Each area has its own will and must be aligned to God's will.

2.   Each area must be dealt with alone with God's grace.

3.   Jesus mastered each area as our example.

You see, Hebrews 4:14-16 states:

Therefore, since we have a great high priest who has gone through the heavens, Jesus the Son of God, let us hold firmly to the faith we profess. For we do not have a high priest who is unable to sympathize with our weaknesses, but we have one who has been tempted in every way, just as we are—yet was without sin. Let us then approach the throne of grace with confidence, so that we may receive mercy and find grace to help us in our time of need.

Jesus purged the will of his flesh in the wilderness, the will of his soul in the Garden of Gethsemane and the will of his spirit on the cross. In like manner we, as believers, must surrender these individual areas of will by submitting these areas to the purging process.

Chapter 2

Definition of a Heavy Call

What is the call of God?

Now that you understand that you are called and the call is a direct mandate from your Creator, God will motivate you to fulfill your call. I want to deliberate for few moments on expressing to you exactly what a heavy call is. I also want to explain to you various types of calls established by God.

The call of God prefaces everything in your life. It is an authoritative command from God which is meant to direct the believers to perform a certain function. If you are a believer, then you can be expected to be "called" into some type of service. The call of God can also be defined as an "invitation to come" or "to be roused from sleep". Romans 13:11 echoes the urgency of the call of God:

"And that, knowing the time, that now it is high time to awake out of sleep: for now is our salvation nearer than when we believed."

I have a great affinity for military service and the millions of servicepersons who volunteer for military duty. I gained this appreciation as an Army recruit at basic training at Fort Sill field artillery base in Lawton, Oklahoma. In August 2001, I arrived in Oklahoma eager to be equipped. The anticipation of transforming myself from a citizen to a soldier was quickly replaced with horrified anger from the terrorism attacks of September 11, 2001. My platoon first became aware of this tragedy as we returned from a field artillery demonstration. As we boarded our bus to return to our dormitory, the infuriated expressions on our drill sergeants soon became incensed words that we, as basic training recruits, weren't yet prepared for. "Get ready, we're going to war".

The proud, yet harsh reality was that we were soldiers indeed and when we signed our allegiance to the military, we signed on for just an occasion as this.

The fact that God has called you shouldn't be a surprise. When God calls you He is pressing you into divine services for His Kingdom. Although you may not feel prepared to answer the call, it is important that you do so you can begin to know God and He can reveal Himself in you and to you.

Answering the Call of God

Have you ever had an important message to relay to someone, only to be frustrated by not being able to get in contact with that person? Have you ever experienced being in a conversation with someone who appears to be listening only to have them drift off in the middle of your dialogue? Is the act of someone ignoring you particularly irritating?

Many times God is attempting to call us only to receive a "busy" signal, a disinterested person, or someone who flat out ignores the assigned mission. Yet still, there are those who simply do not recognize God's voice when He calls. A prime example of the latter occurs in 1 Samuel 3:1-7:

 The boy Samuel ministered before the LORD under Eli. In those days the word of the LORD was rare; there were not many visions. One night Eli, whose eyes were becoming so weak that he could barely see, was lying down in his usual place. The lamp of God had not yet gone out, and Samuel was lying down in the temple of the LORD, where the ark of God was. Then the LORD called Samuel. Samuel answered, "Here I am." And he ran to Eli and said, "Here I am; you called me." But Eli said, "I did not call; go back and lie down." So he went and lay down. Again the LORD called, "Samuel!" And Samuel got up and went to Eli and said, "Here I am; you called me." "My son," Eli said, "I did not call; go back and lie down." Now Samuel did not yet know the LORD: The word of the LORD had not yet been revealed to him.

I have no doubt that a great amount of believers today are of an obedient and willing heart and desire nothing more than to answer God's resounding call. Yet many have not distinguished God's voice enough to recognize who it is calling them. Therefore, they cannot accurately answer the call. 1 Corinthians 14:10 reads:

There are, it may be, so many kinds of voices in the world, and none of them is without signification.

Only investing meaningful time in the Word of God and prayer will allow you to understand the distinctive voice of God.

1 Samuel 3:8-10 gives the believer a synopsis of the correct way to answer:

"And the LORD called Samuel again the third time. And he arose and went to Eli, and said, Here am I; for thou didst call me. And Eli perceived that the LORD had called the child. Therefore Eli said unto Samuel, Go, lie down: and it shall be, if he call thee, that thou shalt say, Speak, LORD; for thy servant heareth. So Samuel went and lay down in his place. And the LORD came, and stood, and called as at other times, Samuel, Samuel. Then Samuel answered, Speak; for thy servant heareth."

There are two critical points for you to ascertain from this passage.

1.   God's call of Samuel was continuous.

2.   God used Eli to provide appropriate and necessary counsel to redirect God.

The first thing you must settle within yourself is that, regardless of whether you decide to answer the call of God, it will never go away. Romans 11:29 tells us, "For God's gifts and his call are irrevocable." People often find themselves dissatisfied with their career or other personal situations because they have never responded (or responded accurately) to the call. This tends to lead people to return to a place where they think God is leading them, only to discover they are mistaken. I implore you to advance your life beyond what you think and ascend to a state of self-knowing through God's revelation. God's will for you is that you know for certain what your calling is and you can only do so through His revelation. Ephesians 1:17 declares, "I keep asking that the God of our Lord Jesus Christ, the glorious Father, may give you the Spirit of wisdom and revelation, so that you may know him better."

 Secondly, when God calls you, He will authorize and position someone who can:

a)   Verify your call.

b)   Counsel you in your call.

Throughout scripture there are many examples of God designating someone to verify and confirm the call of another individual. Some examples include:

Old Testament   New Testament

Melchizedek and Abraham – Gen. 19:17 Jesus confirmed by John the Baptist – John 3:11

Pharoah confirms Joseph – Gen 41:38

Jesus confirmed by Elizabeth – Luke 1:46-53

Moses & Joshua – Dt 31:1-7

Jesus confirmed by Zechariah – Luke 1:67-80

Saul confirmed as king – 1 Samuel 12:12-14

Jesus confirmed by Simeon – Luke 2:28-35

Samuel confirms David – 1 Samuel 16:1-13

Jesus confirmed by Ananias and Paul - Acts 11:17

Paul and Timothy – 2 Timothy 1:3-9

God used Eli to give Samuel instruction as to how to answer God's call. Samuel was instructed first to go and lie down. By instructing Samuel to wait in a still, solitary place, Eli was prepping Samuel to receive all of God's instruction. In our "get up and go" world, we have incorporated a flawed mentality that activity equates to accomplishment. This is erroneous, however, because the truth is amiss activity equates to incomplete accomplishment. The e next instruction given by Eli to Samuel was to listen. I can truthfully say that the older I become, the more of an active listener I have become also. Listening involves more than simply hearing someone. We hear sounds all the time that do not necessarily require our attention. Listening is a more aggressive type of hearing characterized by a greater degree of attention to the information being relayed. Listening to God requires total solitary attentiveness in order to accurately receive what God is saying to you.

A Heavy Call

"Weighing a relatively large amount, and thus difficult to carry or move"

I consider myself an avid runner. The fluidity of my running directly correlates to several factors. You see, I have resigned myself to the fact that although I may never be a world class runner, I have acquired enough ability to solidly achieve my personal running goals. Everyone can't run like I do, and, in turn, I can't expect to run like anyone else. Much like other fitness and health food gurus, I struggle to lose enough weight to maintain a healthy lifestyle and keep fi t enough to enjoy my running hobby. The more weight I carry on my body the more arduous the task of running becomes. In the same manner, the enormity of your call will weigh on you the longer you delay. Your wait becomes a weight. The immovable, irrevocable call of God remains and as such becomes increasingly heavier until you decide to answer it. By understanding these basic premises – who is calling you and how to answer your call--you are prepared to move completely in the type of call to which you've been assigned.

Types of Call

As you can imagine, there are many different types of calls. Answering your "God call" doesn't mean you are necessarily being sent into a ministry career, but, rather, you are choosing to submit to the vocation of divine service. You will know what you are called to do. Although you may feel inadequate to pursue your call, God has already imputed in your make up the components necessary to fulfill your call. Your response may not always be to a single area but may, in fact, require you to spiritually multitask several divinely appointed assignments.

The Call to Salvation

Acts 2:38-39 "Peter replied, "Repent and be baptized, every one of you, in the name of Jesus Christ for the forgiveness of your sins. And you will receive the gift of the Holy Spirit. The promise is for you and your children and for all who are far off —for all whom the Lord our God will call."

I don't want to be presumptuous and assume that everyone reading this book is a Christian. There are two genuine reasons why God chose me to the ministry and, ultimately, we all share these same responsibilities. Those purposes are to rescue the lost and bring reformation to the Church. I want to encourage those of you who are reading and never asked Jesus for His salvation to do so. Amidst the births of the innumerable amount churches today, I also want to remind churches of our main mission, which is to save the lost.

The Call to Holiness

The absence of genuine reverence of God permeates our world. God's call to return to holiness is especially crucial for the church. Many people outside of the church refuse to align themselves with the Body of Christ, because of the erosion of traditional, holy Christian values. 2 Corinthians 7:1 states "...let us purify ourselves from everything that contaminates body and spirit, perfecting holiness out of reverence for God."

God's call to holiness is a call to rid ourselves of elements, people, or situations that conflict with His standard of living. Let's be real. The body of Christ is plagued with people who compromisingly allow immoral deeds (especially sexual immorality) to pollute the church. As we grow in our calls we must do so, eliminating impurity and submitting to God's standard of holiness. Thessalonians 4:3-8 is especially clear on the responsibility of holiness. It is of little use to call yourself a Christian if you are going to live any kind of way, because your immoral lifestyle will always impede your growth and call.

The Call to This Hour

Have you ever considered why we were born at this time? God called you for this time, because in His Sovereignty, He established a divine predetermination of your personal destiny. God understood in His omniscience that only you could perform your divine assignment at this stage in history the way that only you can. The people we witness in the Bible who performed tremendous exploits are notable, and I always find it remarkable what they accomplished. Hebrews 11:32-40 provides an account of some of these accomplishments.

"And what more shall I say? I do not have time to tell about Gideon, Barak, Samson, Jephthah, David, Samuel and the prophets, who through faith conquered kingdoms, administered justice, and gained what was promised; who shut the mouths of lions, quenched the fury of the flames, and escaped the edge of the sword; whose weakness was turned to strength; and who became powerful in battle and routed foreign armies. Women received back their dead, raised to life again. Others were tortured and refused to be released, so that they might gain a better resurrection. Some faced jeers and flogging, while still others were chained and put in prison. They were stoned; they were sawed in two; they were put to death by the sword. They went about in sheepskins and goatskins, destitute, persecuted and mistreated— the world was not worthy of them. They wandered in deserts and mountains, and in caves and holes in the ground. These were all commended for their faith, yet none of them received what had been promised. God had planned something better for us so that only together with us would they be made perfect."

I am in awe of figures of faith (whether they are historical or present day faith juggernauts). I realize that each one's individual purpose was meant solely for him in the hour to which God called them to. Although emulating a person's faith is commendable, I recognize that the hour to which we are called and the duties which we perform are equally relevant to the fulfillment of God's eternal purpose. Be yourself in this hour, and know that your contribution to the kingdom is as important as anyone else's call to the ministry.

Call to Order

Isaiah 44:6-7 reads," Thus saith the LORD the King of Israel, and his redeemer the LORD of hosts; I am the first, and I am the last; and beside me there is no God.

 And who, as I, shall call, and shall declare it, and set it in order for me, since I appointed the ancient people? and the things that are coming, and shall come, let them shew unto them."

Some people are not satisfied with serenity. Instead, they live a chaotic existence accentuated by riotous living. I personally know people who are not satisfied unless something negative is occurring in their life. I make it a practice to leave those types of people alone, because misery loves company and I refuse to be the company they keep!

God is of order, and, as such, He wants order to be prevalent in both the church and our individual lives. Disorder is characterized by confusion and trouble. A life that is in a constant state of flux is not what God intended. Churches that are out of sorts are not beneficial to the Kingdom of God. Both individuals and churches who fail to deal with disorder run the risk of allowing compromise in their lives.

Call to Prayer

I hardly recall what we, as a society, did prior to the advent of the cellular phone. I don't know about you, but both my familial and business lifelines are tied to my direct connection to this device. Without it, I would be disconnected from the interaction in which I engage on a daily basis. My profit and flexibility would suffer tremendously. My investment in my cell phone (or I should say my monthly, recurring bill) is a minor inconvenience to pay as opposed to the benefits of usage it yields.

Jesus advocated, "That men should always pray and not faint", and Paul in his benediction to the Thessalonian church urged us to "pray without ceasing". When prayer is absent from the life of believers, it often occurs because there is a disregard for the benefits that prayer produces. Continual prayer yields continual connection to God. Jesus would often retreat to a place of solitary prayer. He had to stay connected to the power and presence of God. Prayer also returns a yield of inner strength that a believer draws from in time of urgency. The body of Christ suffers immensely from a lack of substantial prayer. Thus we are often disconnected to God and disconcert with each other. Paul again reminds us to pray for each other in Ephesians 6:18:

"And pray in the Spirit on all occasions with all kinds of prayers and requests. With this in mind, be alert and always keep on praying for all the saints." You may be called to any combination of the callings listed above. I am not suggesting that we cannot participate in all these areas, I am simply saying that if any of these areas are not established, then God will prompt you to spend more time with Him in these various types of calls.

Chapter 3

Principles of a Lonely Walk

"When you close your doors, and make darkness within, remember never to say that you are alone; nay, God is within. And what need have they of light to see what you are doing."

Epictetus

Toe the Line

As you can imagine, life as a soldier in a basic training is never easy. If you have a passive work ethic, then the grumblings of an overbearing drill sergeant can be particularly annoying. My decision to enter military life was primarily based on two reasons. The first was because I was at a stage of renovation and renewal in my life and I needed to deal with me. Broken relationships and unfulfilled personal accomplishments had become a mainstay for me. It was so frustrating, knowing that God had blessed me with a ton of untapped ability, but...life...

I had become the perfect example of what was described back in my seventh grade science class – potential energy. You see, science teaches us there is a distinct difference between potential energy and kinetic energy. Potential energy is that energy which is stored within a body of matter until it is released. Kinetic energy is energy that is in motion. Like many of you reading this book, my frustration was based on my untapped ability placed within me by my Creator. The frustration over wanting more of my life led me to make the decision to walk toward God in a more kinetic manner. I chose the solitary recesses of military training because I knew I would have to confront my unfulfillment, lack of accomplishment and untapped energy head on.

The second reason for entering military life may surprise you. I actually wanted the discipline and daily rigor which military life imposes on an individual. As a self-admitted underachiever, I understood the military schedule I would endure would be a difficult one. Days quickly turned to nights during basic training, as the persistent drill sergeant filled our every moment with physically and/or mentally draining functions. Our day began in the wee hours of the morning. We had to learn quickly to "toe the line", which meant do as we were instructed exactly when we were instructed. If we failed to do so, then we literally would have to "toe the line". The literal expression "toe the line" is derived from exercises conducted by the recruits as we were ordered to stand in a delegated section of our cold, linoleum floor with our toes parallel to the nearest segmented floor line. Often, we would be forced to perform various physical routines. Little did we know that we were slowly and methodically being reshaped into finely tuned, disciplined instruments of warfare. The meticulous process of becoming confident in our physical strength and mental acumen been obtained by the recruits unknowingly.No one can choose to accept your call for you, and hardly anyone will choose to walk with you. Many of you have not reached your untapped potential and you are at a stage in your life where you are

a)   Already walking alone.

b)   Designated by God to be alone.

c)   Presently alone due to dictating circumstances.

 For those who are already alone, only you know why your heart is considering doing so. For those who know God as ordered you to be alone, it's time to do so. And for those who have circumstances surrounding your life, it is a must that you do so. Whatever category applies to your situation, you must establish for your own sanctity several guidelines that will allow you to "toe the line" towards your call.

Be Alone, Not Lonely!

The most difficult part about walking alone is the loneliness you feel. Loneliness and being alone are two different entities altogether. Loneliness is characterized by feeling alone; having feelings of being alone or sad. It is derived from being isolated or rarely visited, lacking companionship, aid or encouragement. Alone means that you are "without any other person or thing nearby". Loneliness is based on emotions, while being alone is a state or condition. Just because you've chosen to be alone, doesn't mean you have to be lonely. Your heavy call will often feel lonely, but the reality of your walk is that you are just without the presence of people or things. Consider the example of David in Psalms 25:16:

"The LORD confides in those who fear him; he makes his covenant known to them. My eyes are ever on the LORD, for only he will release my feet from the snare. Turn to me and be gracious to me, for I am lonely and afflicted."

David understood quite well that he was lonely during his manifold tribulations. He never denied his true feelings he simply expressed them to God Himself. It was because of David's understanding of his reciprocal covenant relationship with the Lord that he knew that he still had someone even when it appeared that many were against him.

Examining You

The worst loneliness is not to be comfortable with yourself.

Mark Twain

The discovery of your self-worth during your lonely walk can be as excruciating as standing on the "toe line". I know that many of you struggle with self-worth issues, as well as trying to determine what exactly your capability is. The e process is excruciating because you must come to grips with who you are and who you are not. You have to determine where you have been, where you are presently, and where you are headed in life. Honesty starts from within and without it you will never be able to achieve a sincere overview of your life. Honest movement toward critical self-examination can save you from yourself. Looking at David's life we can again highlight the pattern we should follow for self-examination.

Psalm 139:30:

Search me, O God, and know my heart; test me and know my anxious thoughts. David understood that it was God and God alone who assisted him in understanding the true intentions of His will. Despite David's ambition to be forever pleasing in God's sight there were major character flaws David had to confront. David needed to save himself from himself. God rewarded David for the faithfulness marred by challenges, controversy, and triumph. David emerged from his origins as an obscure shepherd boy through his succession to royalty. Along the way David was anointed king, killed Goliath the giant, survived Saul's assassination attempts, won numerous victories, withstood the ridicule of his wife, the rejection of his brothers, banishment from Saul's kingdom, and overcame a civil war to become the king of Israel and Judah. Yet, David forgot about God's fantastic deliverance, and instead became wrapped up in a conspiracy to commit murder so he could engage in an adulterous affair with another man's wife. Instead of trying to cover up his felonious intent, David understood the ramifications of his wrong and immediately repented. If David didn't had the heart to self-examine his evil intentions, he could have faced the distinct possibility of a divine death sentence.

In our individual lives we often prefer travel down a major interstate of compromise rather than adjourning to a "spiritual rest stop", where we can objectively assess the good, the bad and the ugly decisions we have to make in our lives. Like King David, we have received an abundant overflow of blessings that we take for granted and if we are not careful to be honest about some things, what we fail to examine will ultimately result in our compromise and demise.

You have an excellence in you very few know about. You have a greatness that other people can't determine. I have yet to meet a person who was not in some degree self-seeking. Being self-seeking is not always negative, in fact the whole purpose for God leading you to your heavy call is so you can seek fulfillment of yourself. Being self-seeking is only negative when you use someone else's talents and resources without giving that person the acknowledgement of their contribution to your life. See, I know you have greatness in you because God is no respecter of persons. What he performs in one person's life, he certainly can do in another's. You should know you are great simply because God has told you. And if you don't know then I am here to tell you how great you are. It doesn't really matter what people think about you. What really matters is that you understand God, who is great, could not have created you without creating you to be great as well.

No one other than you will ever know the depth of your relationship with God, nor the magnitude of the tasks you are about to accomplish. And you know what? I have come to the understanding that because people are so self-seeking they don't need to know. Those of you who can remember ever being mistreated, do you think you would have received such mistreatment if those persons really understood the end result of your greatness? I hardly doubt that the religious constituency in Jesus' time would have rejected his words if they understood *He was the Word*. Nor do I think that Potiphar would have been so quick to imprison Joseph had it been revealed to him that Joseph would one day be his commanding officer. People often fail to perceive the greatness in others because they are so absorbed in their own existence. They recognize certain attributes of your greatness, but will hardly give the greatness in you the credit you deserve. Extrinsic perception of another person's life can only be accurately performed if the one being viewed is in the heart of the viewer.

Therefore, it would be wise for you to keep hidden the talents and greatness while you're alone with God. You are headed somewhere in your life that no one else can go.

Chapter 4

The Wilderness Experience

When you understand that you are called by God, often the first place he will lead you is into the wilderness. Literally, a wilderness is a barren, uncultivated, uninhabited area of land. Sometimes a wilderness is deliberately perceived to be just that – a place of barren desolation. A wilderness is a location predetermined by God to be a habitation of initial surrender. I call the wilderness my personal station of rescue and reformation. It is not unusual to have multiple wilderness experiences throughout your life, nor is it remarkable to that God is leading you to a place of barrenness.

Keeping It Real

One of the reasons why I favor the apostle Paul is because of his sincerity in dealing with his transformation from being a persecutor to a preacher. Let's face it, not everyone would have "kept it real" like Paul. I am convinced that many in the Body of Christ impede their own growth because of an overwhelming prevalence to refrain from "keeping it real". If your life is messed up, it's just messed up. If you're in a bad situation, it's just a bad situation. I have never understood why people are not open with God. I often marvel at the wealth of understanding Paul received directly from God. This process of understanding didn't come for Paul because of his academic knowledge or religious affiliations. It occurred because Paul came to the realization (after his conversion) that he needed to confer with another human about the direction of his call. This noble conclusion led Paul to go to a place most familiar for most believers – the wilderness.

You must surrender yourself to God and the duration of His process extends throughout your life. The desolation of a wilderness experience is designed to do just that – help your surrender while drawing you closer to God. In other words, because you have a call on your life you will at some point enter the wilderness experience. There are different types of wilderness and my wilderness experiences may differ from yours. Let's distinguish what these types are.

The Corrective Wilderness

Numbers 32:8-13 reads:

"This what your fathers did when I sent them from Kadesh Barnea to look over the land. After they went up to the Valley of Eshcol and viewed the land, they discouraged the Israelites from entering the land the LORD had given them. The LORD's anger was aroused that day and he swore this oath: 'Because they have not followed me wholeheartedly, not one of the men twenty years old or more who came up out of Egypt will see the land I promised on oath to Abraham, Isaac and Jacob not one except Caleb son of Jephunneh the Kenizzite and Joshua son of Nun, for they followed the LORD wholeheartedly.' The LORD's anger burned against Israel and he made them wander in the desert forty years, until the whole generation of those who had done evil in his sight was gone."

If you are a parent then you know and appreciate the value of a behavior modification technique we refer to as "time out". Time out is generally instituted for a child when he disobeys a directive given to him by his parent. The purpose of a "time out" is to withdraw the child from his malevolent course because the parent is aware that if the behavior continues, ultimately the disobedience will result in an action that is destructive or harmful to something, someone or even the child himself. The shoulder of responsibility to correct the child is upon the parent because obviously the parent knows more about the impending result of the child's conduct. Certainly, children often disappoint their parents with their actions. Often we want to give our children the best in life, but we refrain from giving them things because they disobey. God had every right to be angry with the children of Israel. After he miraculously delivered them from Egypt, supernaturally sustained them in the wilderness, he was prepared to fulfill his promise to them of letting them enter the land of Canaan. The children of Israel failed to realize that God wanted to give them the very best of everything. They began to exhibit a pattern of disobedience and disrespect for what God had achieved for them. This pattern continued until the children of Israel provoked God to remove them from their course and place them in an exhaustive "time out" for forty years. God was so angry with the children of Israel that a simple journey of three days to their promised land became a forty year demonstration of God's correction.

It is no surprise that many people today are wandering in a spiritual wilderness. There are those of you whom seem to have never reached your destination in life. You know what I mean- the place that God intended for you to be. It could very well be that God has allowed you to wander as a corrective action for your disobedience to His directive. Although it is punitive, it's also a measure of God's love. Proverbs 3:11 testifies to this fact. It states, "For whom He loves He chastens."

God will allow you to remain in your corrective wilderness until you faithfully submit to what He has called you to do.

Wilderness of Worship

Exodus 5:1 tells us:

"Afterward Moses and Aaron went to Pharaoh and said, "This is what the LORD, the God of Israel, says: 'Let my people go, so that they may hold a festival to me in the desert."

God will often call you out of a situation to a solitary place of worship. Think about it, when a great many of you are delivered it's often a significant deliverance from dire situations, drama or trauma.

The first thing on God's agenda is not to give you a house, car or money as many in the contemporary church preach. God's first purpose for placing you in the wilderness to worship. Wilderness worship is different that corporate worship. It involves an arrival of consciousness to the major facts surrounding your deliverance. The fact that you need to worship in and of itself should be enough to stimulate your desire to worship. After 400 years of bondage the first thing God did was call the children of Israel to the wilderness to worship him.

Led into Wilderness

"to him who led his people through the desert, His love endures forever." Psalm 136:16.

God will not only lead you to the wilderness, He will lead you through the wilderness. It is never God's intention to lead you to a barren place and to have you remain in that barren place. For those of you who know that you are in a wilderness experience, understand it is only temporary. God has every intention on leading you out. How long you remain in the wilderness depends on how long it takes you to submit to his leading. God's leading must become the rule for your life as opposed to the exception.

Romans 8:14 states, "because those who are led by the Spirit of God are sons of God." God, by his spirit will directly lead you to the wilderness. Matthew 4:8 states, "then Jesus was led up of the Spirit into the wilderness to be tempted of the devil". What is of particular note are the words "to be". These words suggest that there was a purpose why Jesus was led into the wilderness. Please be cognizant that God will always designate a "to be" for your wilderness experience, and it is the Spirit of God that leads you to that designation.

Make no mistake about it, you will be led by something. You will be led by God, your own being (body, soul or spirit), or by the devil. Whomever you are led by will determine your success or failure in life. People sometimes fail to understand that because Jesus was in all points tempted like we are, *He could have failed*. Jesus knew he was being led by the Spirit into the wilderness, so he willingly submitted himself to 40 days of sacrificial fasting in order to accomplish the task of defeating Satan's temptations. Once you understand that you are being led into the wilderness you must be willing to do whatever is sacrificially necessary to be successful in the wilderness. This could mean extensive praying, extensive fasting, or interpersonal exile, but understand there will be sacrifice involved. Most people don't want to sacrifice, which is why people end up in a state of wilderness, stagnation – never making it to their promised land.

Wilderness of Refuge

Have you ever been in some trouble you were sure how to escape? Have you ever been so angry at someone that you wanted to seriously retaliate? Have you ever needed a break from it all? Remember the old

"Calgon, take me away" commercial? It contained a humorous clip of a woman who was so overwhelmed with daily activities that she simply wanted to be expeditiously and safely removed from her troubles. She was asking for refuge. A refuge is an environment that is designed in order to provide protection and shelter in difficult times.

Psalm 46:1 declares, "God is our refuge and strength, a very present help in trouble."

I am often amazed at the amount of Christians who won't run to God in difficult or trying circumstances. God will often call you to a quiet place in order to remove you from danger or trouble. Not only did David know God as being merciful, he also knew God as refuge for all David's troubles.

Psalm 31:1-4 tells us, "In you, O LORD, I have taken refuge; let me never be put to shame; deliver me in your righteousness. Turn your ear to me, come quickly to my rescue; be my rock of refuge, a strong fortress to save me. Since you are my rock and my fortress, for the sake of your name lead and guide me. Free me from the trap that is set for me, for you are my refuge.

David understood that in order for him to receive deliverance he would have to trust God completely for a miraculous occurrence. Some of you are in such dire straits that only divine assistance will allow you to make it. There are also those of you would have suffered at the hands of someone and you would like nothing better than to get them back. Still, some of you just need a break from everyday trials of life. If you can identify with one of these categories, don't' be surprised if God is calling you to a quiet place, so He can be your refuge. God will often remove you from a situation, so that he can protect you from trouble, the anger you are experiencing, or just give you a break and allow Him to be a refuge for you. Even if you are the reason why the trouble is occurring, if you trust Him he will be the refuge you need.

 Moses, in his haste to be a deliverer for the enslaved children of Israel, killed an Egyptian and fled into the wilderness. Little did he know he would one day be the deliverer he feebly attempted to be by himself. Sometimes, when we go through life, we make catastrophic mistakes.

God is merciful in that he can turn around our worst mistakes, and make those mistakes miracles.

Wilderness of Revelation

"I keep asking that the God of our Lord Jesus Christ, the glorious Father, may give you the Spirit of wisdom and revelation, so that you may know him better." Ephesians 1:17

There is a major difference between arrogant people and confident people. Arrogant people are generally under the notion they are far more advanced in some respect or another than other people and this regard is usually displayed in some expressive from of contempt toward others. Confident people are different, though. Confident people generally have assurance in their ability to achieve. Some people exhibit both confidence and arrogance, while others lack both. I have found that the Body of Christ is littered with persons who have become arrogant about their status, position or title in the Body of Christ. Truly arrogant people annoy me to no end, but truly confident people are admirable. Arrogant people (especially in the church) and I do not really interact well together, because I generally feel an unction to respond to their arrogance by revealing to them just how important they are not. Usually my unction is tempered by the Holy Spirit prohibiting me from giving them the tongue lashing they may richly deserve. You know, you can tell when people are "feeling" themselves too much. They usually have a repulsive expression (verbally or otherwise) that suggests, "Don't you know who I am?" "Don't you know who I am?" people are everywhere today, especially in church. A great deal of ministries are formed today on the basis that the presiding officials want you to know who they are. I have personally been witness to services where the emphasis was on who the minister is, as opposed to who Jesus is. "Don't you know who I am?" people will never get far with God because he desires the church to contrast arrogance with a true spirit of humility.

True Revelation

True revelation from God was never intended to lift someone to a plateau of arrogance. Instead true revelation from God is given from the Almighty in order that you might understand and know Jesus. It keeps you grounded on a plain of humility. It's pretty difficult to think arrogantly of yourself when Jesus is revealed in you, because you understand that without Jesus you wouldn't accomplish anything. When you receive true revelation from God it humbles you and gives you confidence; it should never make you more arrogant. I often wonder how the religious leaders of Jesus' day could arrogantly defy Jesus. It's pretty simple: Jesus had every desire to reveal Himself to all, but only a limited number of people actually believed in His revelation. The same holds true today. Although many are immersed in a wealth of knowledge about God, very few people spend enough time with God to let Him reveal Himself to you and through you.

I am certain that someone (perhaps with a title, mega congregation, multipurpose facility, or multimillion dollar business) is reading this saying, "Hmmm...I know God has revealed Himself to me." But to that person I would say, the fact you think that you are satisfied with the revelation God has given you is evidence that God has not finished working on your ego. I am never satisfied with one revelation from God. True revelation always leaves desiring more of Revealer. No one has truly "arrived" and everyone needs some type of continuous revelation from God. You, in fact, need a wilderness revelation more than anyone because, like Paul prior to his conversion, you think you are "advanced in what you know". God will often bring you to the wilderness because there is a revelation He wants to give you specific c to your situation. The path to the wilderness of revelation is not always easy, but the revelation you will receive from God will always be just compensation from difficulties you endure. Sometimes, your most painful experiences are opportunities for God to truly reveal himself to you.

Genesis 21:9-19 is a powerful example of God's revelation to you in the wilderness:

And Sarah saw the son of Hagar the Egyptian, which she had born unto Abraham, mocking. Wherefore she said unto Abraham, Cast out this bondwoman and her son: for the son of this bondwoman shall not be heir with my son, even with Isaac. And the thing was very grievous in Abraham's sight because of his son. And God said unto Abraham, Let it not be grievous in thy sight because of the lad, and because of thy bondwoman; in all that Sarah hath said unto thee, hearken unto her voice; for in Isaac shall thy seed be called.   And also of the son of the bondwoman will I make a nation, because he is thy seed. And Abraham rose up early in the morning, and took bread, and a bottle of water, and gave it unto Hagar, putting it on her shoulder, and the child, and sent her away: and she departed, and wandered in the wilderness of Beersheba. And the water was spent in the bottle, and she cast the child under one of the shrubs. And she went, and sat her down over against him a good way off, as it were a bow shot: for she said, let me not see the death of the child. And she sat over against him, and lift up her voice, and wept. And God heard the voice of the lad; and the angel of God called to Hagar out of heaven, and said unto her, What aileth thee, Hagar? Fear not; for God hath heard the voice of the lad where he is. Arise, lift up the lad, and hold him in thine hand; for I will make him a great nation. And God opened her eyes, and she saw a well of water; and she went, and filled the bottle with water, and gave the lad drink."

It was in Hagar and Ishmael's desperate state that God revealed himself to Hagar. Many times, as with Hagar, God will reveal his plan to you in your desperation. I told you before that I went through the process of homelessness. Like Hagar and millions of others who have been through it, I had very little provision. Although everyone's reasons for being homeless are different, the sting of not being able to lie in your own bed, retrieve you own mail, or eat from your kitchen is a sting that has been stored by more people than you think. It was during my desperate time that Jesus revealed Himself to me. "Darian, I have called you to rescue and reform. But you have made so many mistakes, that I have to first reform your life."

It was in my most desperate hour of loneliness, despair, and loss that I received the greatest revelation specific to my life. Like me, God wants to rescue many of you from your despair and reform you in the wilderness of revelation.

The Wilderness of Surrender

Those long, simmering hot days of basic training gave me a tremendous amount of insight about the tactics of war. The commanding officers were always stressing to the recruits the seriousness of our training, especially with the onset of the war on terrorism. The relentless nature of the training was always geared toward making us better prepared to engage our enemies and force them to yield to our advances. The purpose of war is to forcefully resolve a dispute. In war there must be a victor and someone must lose. Being a soldier, I learned the tenacity necessary needed to be victorious when there is an enemy in front of you. When you are forced to engage an enemy you must force that enemy either to surrender or perish. Losing is not an option because your loss will cost you dearly – and in war it will even cost you your life.

When God calls you to the wilderness of surrender, He knows you are in a war. The key opponents in this war are God's will versus your very own will. You know, the first thing that Jesus did when He went to the wilderness was to surrender His flesh to God's will. He did so because He knew in order to war with the devil, He first had to war with Himself. Many people in the Body of Christ attempt to forge a full scale invasion of the devil without first battling the enemy within you – the flesh.

I am astounded by the eradication of moral values in today's church. The eradication of values extends from the pulpit to the front door. I have never been surprised at the moral lawlessness that exists in the world, because we know fully what the world is capable of doing. However, when this lawlessness extends to the church, it should be of great concern. Rampant immorality exists everywhere in the church because there is little or no surrender on a personal or corporate level. I stress the importance of the declining morality in the church, because it is based in the unwillingness of many to surrender themselves to the will of God. The habitation of initial surrender is where God wants you to combat your flesh. It is absolutely critical to win this internal conflict because it determines your success in God. If your flesh wins, God's will for your life loses, and if God's will for your life wins your flesh will lose. This type of surrender requires you to submit your flesh to God and yes, it does require intensive fasting and praying.

The wilderness experience is far from trivial and these types of wilderness experiences only serve to strengthen you as you walk alone towards your call. The truth is, everyone in the Israelite camp did not survive the forty year wilderness experience, nor will everyone in today's society partake in the discipline needed to survive in the wilderness. For those of you who do, expect to be alone, expect to survive, and most importantly expect it to be temporary and greatly rewarding.

Chapter 5

Great Leaders Who Walked Alone

"...But the great man is he who in the midst of the world, keep with perfect sweetness in the independence of solitude."

Ralph Waldo Emerson

Tunnel Vision

I often reminisce about the origins of my faith. My earliest memories bring me back to a time where my world consisted of a mother and a stepfather who loved and sheltered me from the chaotic surroundings that accompany low-income living in an inner city project area. I wasn't aware of poverty or lack, my interests were in the daily recreation of my neighborhood. My parents always tried to promote an environment of protection away from the increasingly troublesome area of crime and degradation.

We were poor, but I never knew it because instead of allowing me to identify with my surroundings, my parents only allowed me to experience the depth of their love and not the destitution that surrounded them. Although I have since discovered long lost sisters and a brother, I was raised as an only child. My mother would often drag me to Wednesday night Bible studies at Mount Zion A.M.E. Church in Dover, DE. My stepfather was a non-participant in these activities; his interaction with God usually consisted of a few well-placed derogatory God-expletives. The irony was that he would always express a sense of remorse for his failures, and intensely admonish me to focus and envision on accomplishing something tremendous in my life. Little did I know that what my parents had established for me was a safe haven - a place where I would only see the best in life.

Tunnel vision is a condition, "in which peripheral vision is lost or severely limited, so that only objects directly in line with the eyes can be seen." Many people today have become so distracted by every disorder of life, that it's hard to focus on what's really important in your life. I told you that my purpose in the Body of Christ is to rescue and reform and my tunnel vision has me completing that mission. God will often remove your peripheral distractions so that your real purpose will come into line with your tunnel vision. Jesus would often warn the following about worrying about extraneous activities that have nothing to do with your purpose. Luke 10:36-41 illustrates what happens when a lack of tunnel vision is present:

"As Jesus and his disciples were on their way, he came to a village where a woman named Martha opened her home to him. She had a sister called Mary, who sat at the Lord's feet listening to what he said. But Martha was <u>distracted</u> by all the preparations that had to be made. She came to him and asked, "Lord, don't you care that my sister has left me to do the work by myself? Tell her to help me!" "Martha, Martha," the Lord answered, "you are worried and upset about many things,"

Martha was so involved with making preparations for Jesus' visit that Jesus had to tell Martha what the true focus of her vision should have been. Notice that Jesus did not respond to Martha until Martha came to Jesus and asked Jesus to correct what she felt was improper. The decision to eliminate distractions in your life will always come from you. God will allow you to continue wading in peripheral distractions until you decide to fulfill your call. Every great leader has to have tunnel vision. I am not suggesting that you can't handle more than one task. My favorite expression of the 21st century is multitasking. Multitasking occurs when you simultaneously manage more than one project. I am declaring to you that your tunnel vision should umbrella your multiple tasks. The tasks you accomplish should never remove you from divine tunnel vision or your call.

When you comprehend what your tunnel vision is, you are able to stand alone in your heavy call. I remember asking God as a young adult to make me the man that He wanted me to be. It was then that God responded by showing to me those gifts and callings that are designated for my life alone. You see, I can't do what God has called you to do. However, if I am simply the best man, pastor, achiever, counselor, entrepreneur, father, husband, friend, mentor which He has called me to be, I am certain my vision won't be distracted by other miscellaneous and misleading matters. I want to take a moment to illustrate other leaders whom I personally admire leaders who have stood alone in their respective call, and made significant contributions to society.

Old Testament

Abraham, Moses, David

Noah, Sampson, Elijah

Joseph, Deborah, Daniel

New Testament

Peter, Paul

The Early Church

Modern Leaders

Billy Graham, Oral Roberts, Kenneth Hagin,

Rev. Dr. Martin Luther King, Jr.,

Rev. Dr. Martin Luther King Jr. in a Birmingham, Alabama jail in 1963

Bishop Thomas Jakes

Abraham- the father of faith, Abraham heard and responded to God's call to leave his father's house and go a place he had never been and do things which had never been done. Abraham was used by God to establish covenant in the earth.

Noah- despite enduring harsh criticism and ridicule Noah stood alone when God called him to build the ark.

Joseph- Joseph held to his faith and dreams. Despite the loneliness and anger he surely must have endured during his banishment from his family and imprisonment at the hands of Potiphar. Joseph to a place of honor in the land of Egypt and forgiveness with his family.

Moses- Humbly and reluctantly accepted the call to challenge Pharoah and deliver the children of Israel out of bondage- withstood the harsh criticism of the people of Israel. Moses had to cope with the enormous task of leading the children of Israel into Canaan.

Sampson- Single handedly took the Philistine nation and stood alone in death after being betrayed by Delilah.

Deborah- prophetess and judge over Israel.

David-Called as a child to be King over Israel, David became much more than a king. He was a warrior, a prophet, and exemplified courage to stand alone against Goliath when no one else was willing to fight Goliath, the giant. His life is a tremendous example of how to dialogue with God, especially when you are alone.

Elijah- One of the greatest prophets. Stood alone against the tyranny and wickedness of King Ahab and Jezebel.

Daniel, Shadrach, Meshach, Abednego- Challenged immoral and ungodly statutes and stood their ground despite governmental oppression that ordered them to worship other Gods or face punishment by death.

New Testament

Peter- Always the first to respond to Jesus, I consider Peter to have been the main risk taker of the disciples. I believe this because it seemed as if Peter was always the first to speak up. Whether the consequence of his actions were favorable or not, Peter at least had the attitude to try.

Paul- Had to overcome his own shame and others' doubts to relay to the early church the gospel message of inclusion to every person who believed. Also was bold in his correction of the other apostle's treatment of Gentile believers.

The early church- Withstood imprisonment, persecution, mockery, and torture to become an institution of hope and revolution. The sacrifices of the martyrs of yesteryear are why we can stand in congregations today- generally without the same type of suffering the early church rendered and freely preach the gospel.

Great Modern Era Leader

Billy Graham- Armed with God's message of salvation, Billy Graham's messages of hope and inspiration have transformed the lives of millions of persons across the world.

Smith Wigglesworth- One of the leaders of the early 20th century charismatic movement, Wigglesworth operated under a tremendous anointing that displayed awesome signs and wonders and the power of God.

Kenneth Hagin, Sr. - Healed by God of an incurable disease at the age of 17, Kenneth Hagin, Sr. was the most influential teacher of faith of the mid to late 20th century.

Bishop Thomas Jakes- Bishop Jakes has become the most prominent Christian leader of the early 21st century. His genuine message of restoration and self-development has healed many of the turmoil and crisis that life brings.

Marilyn Hickey- A steadfast teacher of the gospel, Marilyn Hickey has traveled the world (often at great risk) to reach the lost with the message of God's eternal life.

There are so many other leaders who walked alone to fulfill their calls. This a general list of some who have personally inspired me and have been trailblazers of faith, while fulfilling their heavy calls.

Chapter 6

I Come to the Garden Alone

(The Second Surrender)

Psalm 131:2:

"Surely, I have calmed and quieted my soul, like a weaned child with his mother, like a weaned child is my soul within me.

You Got Soul

As recruits start basic training they do so with a braggadocio and sense of pride that they can accomplish anything. I found it almost humorous that my fellow recruits often expressed a youthful ignorance that they were capable of handling any required objective they encountered. I guess because I was older (entered basic training at the age of 29), I knew there were skilled drill sergeants waiting to prey on every wide eyed recruit who dared not to comply with the drill sergeant's orders. The younger recruits were especially vulnerable to the drill sergeant's angry interaction. Many of them were leaving home for the first time. Basic training is designed to break a soldier down to the lowest level of emotional confidence and physical strength. Whenever an individual quits on something, the process of that quitting always begins in the emotional part of you. There were times when we as recruits wanted to continue training but were physically exhausted and there were times when we emotionally were completely drained to the point of resignation.

Five weeks into my training and approximately one month after the horrible destruction of 9/11, I received an overwhelming emotional lift, which would catapult me forward to completion of my basic training. The event was a collegiate football game between Texas Christian University and Army. For the three thousand Fort Sill recruits who attended it was a much needed injection of sorely missed recreation. We entered Texas Christian University as a mighty and marching military ensemble, bellowing in coordinated unison the cadences we had come to know and love. Tears trickled down my eyes. I saw families weeping in both admiration of our presence and remorse over the loss of our fellow countrymen who gave their lives on September 11, 2001.

Honestly, have never been more proud to be an American than in those precious moments...

-TCU vs. Army October 20, 2001 at Texas Christian University. Over 3000 soldiers marched into the stadium.

-Fort Sill soldiers enjoying TCU vs. Army October 20, 2001

I want to take a moment to define for you what your soul is. The soul is defined as "the nonphysical attributes that manifest as consciousness, through feeling, and will and is distinct from the physical body. Another definition says, "Somebody's emotional and moral nature, where the most private parts are hidden". Your soul is the inner and emotional you, the part of you that allows you to express all of the emotions you feel and the decisions you make. People who can't control their soul can't control their emotions. We often witness people making soulish, emotional decisions in their life because they lack soul self-control. A riotous soul is often the main ingredient in the recipe of self-destruction. I am leery of Christians who make soulish emotional decisions as opposed to Spirit led decisions because soul decisions often end up hurting something or someone. Much like basic training, the pressure of life will often place you on the brink of emotional emptiness. Satan often crafts plans to wither away your emotional strength. I don't know about you, but sometimes an emotional shortage can be as taxing as physical challenges.

The Second Surrender

I am extremely fond of the highlighted verse at the beginning of this chapter. David learned an important lesson that all believers must comprehend and incorporate into their own lives. David learned the importance of the process of soul control. The process of soul control occurs when an individual maintains a disciplined emotional existence. Many times when believers go through challenges they have a propensity to "go off". You know, snap the neck, roll the eyes and let whoever or whatever know how you feel. Or they have an emotional outburst that ends up in relationships being forever tainted and severed.

Every sin that has ever knowingly been committed occurred because a lack of soul control was evident.

You learned earlier that in the wilderness, Jesus spent 40 agonizing days fasting in the wilderness in order to surrender his flesh to the will of the Heavenly Father. This the habitation of initial surrender. Although Jesus successfully endured the wilderness experience, he still had to undergo the process of soul surrender. People often successfully complete one phase of their spiritual life only to have other areas that they need to successfully engage. The truth is we are always facing obstacles which challenge our body, soul, or spirit. If a person successfully completes a fast to have more control of their flesh, but still cannot control their temper, it only tells me that person needs more soul control. On the other hand, if that same person is the calmest person in the world, but excessively and gluttonously eats everything in sight, it only discloses the need for more time in the habitation of initial surrender. Jesus' greatest challenge on earth was not surrendering his flesh in the wilderness nor was it the external opposition of Satan on the religious leaders of his day. His greatest opposition was internal – the surrender of what he wanted to do versus the will of His Father. The greatest challenges you face will be those inside of you.

Obviously, the prevailing theme throughout the book is that your call to higher service in God directly correlates to your need to be alone with God. Many people will often attempt to bring people along with them in order to have support for their lonely walk. Yet, the truth of the matter is very few people can identify with the personal journey, challenges and victories you go through. Your spiritual makeup is unique and as such those elements in you that allow to persevere through trauma and drama are different than those you are trying to carry with you. Especially in times of extreme adversity we often find out just who our real supporters are. Being acquainted with you and being familiar with your circumstances does not constitute someone being qualified to endure with you in your lonely walk.

Matthew 26:36 – 45 reads:

Then cometh Jesus with them unto a place called Gethsemane, and saith unto the disciples, Sit ye here, while I go and pray yonder. And he took with him Peter and the two sons of Zebedee, and began to be sorrowful and very heavy. Then saith he unto them, my soul is exceeding sorrowful, even unto death: tarry ye here, and watch with me. And he went a little farther, and fell on his face, and prayed, saying, O my Father, if it be possible, let this cup pass from me: nevertheless not as I will, but as thou wilt. And he cometh unto the disciples, and findeth them asleep, and saith unto Peter, What, could ye not watch with me one hour? Watch and pray, that ye enter not into temptation: the spirit indeed is willing, but the flesh is weak. He went away again the second time, and prayed, saying, O my Father, if this cup may not pass away from me, except I drink it, thy will be done. And he came and found them asleep again: for their eyes were heavy. And he left them, and went away again, and prayed the third time, saying the same words. Then cometh he to his disciples, and saith unto them, Sleep on now, and take your rest: behold, the hour is at hand, and the Son of man is betrayed in the hands of sinners.

In this passage of scripture, Jesus brought His disciples with him to Gethsemane. Having already completed the last supper, Jesus was fully aware that trouble was imminent and his betrayal and death were forthcoming. Knowing this, Jesus brought the disciples with him to Gethsemane to stay with him. Upon arriving at the garden, he brought Peter, James and John deeper into the garden to pray with him. It was at this point Jesus dealt with the anguish of his pending death, seemingly with his support group at his side. Three times Jesus went to confront death and three times Jesus found his same support group disinterested in Jesus' personal agony enough to the point of sleeping. People can stay with you, people can pray with you, and people can even be in close proximity to where you are laboring through your ordeal and still not understand what you are going through. The second surrender, or your soul surrender, requires that you eliminate both a riotous soul and your need to have unnecessary people constantly surrounding you.

Chapter 7

The Useless Opinion of Man

"Public opinion is a permeating influence and it exacts obedience to itself. It requires us to drink other men's thoughts, to speak other men's works, to follow other men's habits."

Walter Bagehot

In the army, I have never met an officer, commissioned or noncommissioned, that was interested in a subordinate's opinion or wanted to receive counsel from a private's point of view about how to accomplish an assigned mission. A good officer is stern in his intention and decisive in his actions. The enormity of responsibility lies squarely on the shoulders of the superior and a misguided opinion will do more harm than good. I want very much to deal with you for a few moments about the need to disregard people's opinions, and deliver yourself from ungodly counsel. I am certain that many of you have probably not differentiated between counsel and opinion, because, when both are conveyed they sound the same. However, they are very different and allow me highlight the difference for you now.

Opinion is defined as "a view, judgment, or appraisal in the mind about a particular matter." People's opinions are based in their experience. Another person's opinion of you is, at best, speculation. Have you ever had the experience of trying to relay an event to someone and before you can ever finish, that person has responded to you with unsolicited advice? As aggravating as it may be, it is equally as unnecessary. A vast majority of time people attempt to relegate their opinion which has based in their own experience to your situation, which is a different experience altogether. Oftentimes, it is like placing a square peg in a round hole; it simply doesn't fit. Even a similar experience is not the same experience.

Counsel is different from opinion. Counsel is solicited advice that an individual seeks regarding a situation. You actually seek out counsel, whereas opinion is often thrust at you. When people ask, "What is your opinion?" they are actually requesting your counsel. God wants you to eliminate ungodly counsel and unsolicited opinion from your life. Both counsel and opinion are at times, warranted but both can be dangerous deterrents to you fulfilling the heavy call on your life. Have your ever met someone who was so absorbed in what other people thought it was hard for them to function? People who are so weighted down by other's opinions and ungodly counsel often limit their ability to succeed, because the weight of others opinions can be taxing and burdensome.

Psalms 1:1 declares, "Blessed is man who walketh not in the counsel of the ungodly..." Christians who receive opinions from non-Christians place themselves at risk of incorporating ideas which are alien to a believer's lifestyle. I'm not saying that other religions don't foster key and at times, profitable knowledge but the true and wisest counsel comes from God. The best way to receive that knowledge is to yield totally to his Spirit. God is not interested in people's opinions or counsel about how to run His Kingdom, and you shouldn't be interested in hearing people's opinions about how to run your life! This not to suggest that you will never receive input from others; it's simply that your ultimate counsel should come from God, and the best opinions are already based in His Word.

Pierre Charron, a famous French philosopher states it best by saying, "The most excellent and divine counsel, the best and most profitable advertisement of all others, but the least practiced is to study and learn how to know ourselves. This the foundation and highway to whatever is good."

The Dangers of Spiritless Opinion and Ungodly Counsel

Beware, Beware, Beware, Beware, Beware...

I am not a fear or fire and brimstone minister, but I must interject a warning and some applicable biblical examples of why it is of the utmost importance to deliver you from opinion and counsel. Please understand that the wrong unsolicited opinion or ungodly counsel can cause you shipwreck or delay opportunities to fulfill your call. Allow me to highlight some of these dangers.

It Will Deter You From the Plan of God.

Oftentimes your closest allies in their zeal for you welfare will state intrusive and misguided opinions about the direction of your life. Consider this example in Matthew 16:21-23 "From that time on Jesus began of explain to his disciples that he must go to Jerusalem and suffer many things at the hands of the elders, chief priests and teachers, of the law and that he must be killed and on the third day raised to life."

Peter took him aside and began to rebuke him "Never, Lord! He said. This shall never happen to you!" Jesus turned and said to Peter "Get behind me, Satan! You are a stumbling block to me; you do not have in mind the things of God, but the things of men."

For years, I have heard people bash Peter as if he morphed into some type of demonic figure, but that's not the case. Jesus was clear in the direction he was to take. Not many days after his pronouncement in this verse He would be crucified for the purpose of reconciling all men back to God. The same way Jesus knew his purpose was to be fulfilled on the cross, we know God's will for our lives. Jesus knew His direction because the Holy Spirit was directing Jesus to the cross. The time you are spending in your lonely walk solidifies your knowledge of the direction of your life. Many of you know what to do with your life, but other's opinions and counsel have deterred you. That's not to suggest that people don't love you, they just love you their way as opposed to the way you need to go for your own life. Peter wasn't the devil, he was one of Jesus' closest allies. In Peter's overzealousness to protect Jesus, he spoke words contrary to the heavy call on Jesus life. People think Jesus was speaking to Peter, but Jesus was actually rebuking the stumbling block Peter hastily spoke from his over eager lips. The people who love you may mean well and you certainly don't have to disown them, but like Jesus you have to decisively speak to their words so your mind is clear and focused on your heavy call.

A source of personal frustration

Job 2:7-10 reads, "So Job went out from the presence of the Lord and afflicted Job with painful sores from the sides of his feet to the top of his head. Then Job took a piece of broken pottery and scraped himself with it as he sat among the ashes. His wife said to him "Are you still holding on to your integrity? Curse God and die!" He replied, "You are talking like a foolish woman. Shall we accept good from God and not trouble?" In all this Job did not sin in what he had said. As if the loss of his cattle, servants and wealth weren't enough, Job was now faced with the painful affliction of sores on his body. I have little patience for people who are intolerant of other people's suffering. You don't know how many times I've heard Christians sit in judgment of others while someone suffers through the agony of tribulation. The truth is the same way that "a great wind" (Job 1:19) blew and it killed Job's children, life's tribulation will blow and destroy a person's life, motivation, family, goals, possessions and dreams. Job's wife gave him miserable counsel at the worst possible moment. In effect, she basically kicked him while he was down.

I often asked myself what kind of spouse would

a)   Curse God

b)   Speak death over your spouse.

Ungodly counsel and unsolicited opinions can often come at the most difficult times and kick us while we are down. People who can use someone else's tribulation as an opportunity to gloat or give foolish, misguided advice are not worth keeping around anyway, as they only serve as a source of personal frustration for your life. In your quiet time you need to examine who loves you enough – who is relevant enough to be there for you through thick and thin.

Ushers a spirit of compromise.

Ungodly counsel and unsolicited opinions can usher a spirit of compromise in your life. People will often attempt to divisively steer you away from God's ordained plan for your life. Remember, anything less than the best is absolutely compromise. Many of you have been persuaded to compromise your value in relational, financial and other vital areas of your life. Compromise kills the call and, understand, it may be a slow death. Those goals that you've been diligently trying to fulfill can slowly and surely dissipate if you allow compromise to circumvent your call. Luke 5:4-8 gives a clear example of how compromise can cost precious time and valuable resources.

"When he finished speaking, he said to Simon, Put out into the deep water, and let your nets for a catch." Simon answered, "Master, we've worked hard all night and haven't caught anything, but because you say so I will let down the net! And when they had done, they enclosed a great multitude of fishes, and their net brake."

Jesus had just finished speaking to the throngs of people who were gathered at the seaside to hear him. There was a two-fold purpose in Jesus' telling Peter to let down his nets. First, Jesus wanted to bless the fishermen for the usage of their vessel. Secondly, because God always confirms the Word which has been spoken, Jesus wanted to demonstrate a powerful miracle of provision for the crowd. God will never use you nor would he have placed a heavy call on your life if he wasn't going to provide for you. And He certainly wants to miraculously illustrate what he can do through your life. Peter didn't realize the enormity of the occasion and instead let down his net. The net was not enough to hold the provision God supplied, because Peter offered his opinion instead of receiving his blessing. Every time I read this passage I want to reach back through the centuries and ask Peter, "Who asked you?" Many of you are wondering "How is God going to bless me?" or "why do I need to do it this way?" or possible even "I know you are God, but if you allow me to put my 2 cents in, I think that…." God doesn't need your opinion, and you don't want anyone in your life who suggests compromise!

Seeds of doubt

The most dangerous type opinion and counsel are those which are deliberately planted in your mind by the devil or others. It is done with the subtle intent to cause chaos in your life. Be clear, your heavy call and the great tasks God has for you will not be endorsed by some and, in fact, make some people feel extremely threatened by you. Everyone doesn't want to see you succeed and some people (even those close to you) may deliberately attempt to seduce you away from what God has called you to do. I have often counseled people who are preparing for marriage, know of a certainty that they are with the right person, but are reluctant to get married because of what someone else thinks about their mate. I have also witnessed people who know they have an awesome call on their life but because someone incorrectly counsels them they delay what is in their heart, and what they know is true. If you are reading this book and you're hesitating to step into an area you know is right for you, my prayer is that you understand that no one can live your life for you, but you.

Archie Ammons, famous philosopher stated it like this:

"Everything is discursive opinion instead of direct experience". In other words, people's opinions are based on their "there experience", instead of your "right now, right here experience.

A perfect example that seeds of doubt are destructive occurs in the book of Daniel 6:7-8

"All the presidents of the kingdom, the governors, and the princes, the counselors, and the captains, have consulted together to establish a royal statute, and to make a firm decree, that whosoever shall ask a petition of any God or man for thirty days, save of thee, O king, he shall be cast into the den of lions. Now, O king, establish the decree, and sign the writing, that it be not changed, according to the law of the Medes and Persians, which altereth not."

I love Daniel because in the face of political opposition and religious suppression he stayed steadfast in his divine discipline. What is most impressive is the fact that Daniel was right where many of you are today – alone. There was a diabolical plot on the behalf of jealous administrators to destroy Daniel regardless of the outcome. People often will concoct plans to hurt you regardless of what the outcome means for you. Notice two things. First, King Darius subjected himself to the ungodly counsel of those who didn't give two hoots about him or Daniel. The danger in Christianity is that we allow people around us who don't really care about us. What's worse is allowing these types of people to express themselves in our lives. Next, notice that even though King Darius had the authority to change Daniel's death decree and everything in him told him to do just that, he compromised the truth in his heart because of the seeds of doubt placed in him by others.

Beware....

The Authoritative You

Every one of you has the authority to put an end to the impact of ungodly counsel and unsolicited opinion in your lives. Basically, if you don't ask an opinion, no one should offer, and if you do seek counsel make sure it is accurate for your life and not based on ungodly doctrine. Anything else can deter you from the plan of God, be a source of personal frustration for you, usher in a spirit of compromise, or sow seeds of doubt. For some of you this may mean letting go of some people, situations. Be strong, be intrinsic, and most always beware!

Proverbs 3:5 reminds us:

"Trust in the Lord with all your heart and lean not to your own understanding. In all your ways acknowledge him and he will make you path straight."

Chapter 8

My God, My God Why Hast Thou Forsaken Me

Questioning God in your lonely walk

Matthew 27:46

And about the ninth hour Jesus cried with a loud voice, saying, Eli, Eli, lama sabachthani? that is to say, My God, my God, why hast thou forsaken me?

"The Romans had their victims stripped and flogged before being crucified in a public place, where they were ridiculed by spectators. Because crucifixion neither damaged internal organs, nor resulted in excessive bleeding, death was slow and painful. Breathing became increasingly difficult, and the victims eventually died through a combination of asphyxiation, shock, hunger and thirst."

John Baker, "The Complete Bible Handbook, An Illustrated Companion"

Ride or Die

Transverse myelitis is not a term people walk around quoting every day. Prior to March, 2004, it was not a phrase I was even familiar with. However, in the early hours of that morning it was a term that changed my life and the life of my thirteen year old daughter (Ericka) forever. Ericka had always been an active child, full of fun and laughter, obedient to even the most trivial parentally assigned tasks. She was my "road dog", always a willing passenger when I traveled. Whenever Daddy wanted to take a trip she was the first of my children to volunteer to be right next to me. We were inseparable. This particular morning, however, Ericka wouldn't be my "road dog" nor would she ride "shotgun" in my passenger seat. Ericka was eagerly preparing to go to school and I kissed her goodbye as I prepared to take a three day business trip to Louisiana (from Virginia Beach, VA). I left her in the more than capable hands of her nanny...

The inexplicable pride that most parents have for their children cannot be described in a few mere words. Truly the joy of seeing a child born, grow up, laugh and cry, emulate and incorporate your ways and habits and reach their full potential is something only a parent can experience. Those of you don't have children can't really identify with the pride a parent has. The love parents have for their children is reciprocated back to the parent with every adoring smile, obedient gesture, and youthfully exuberant behavior. Parents have contentment, when it is well with their children. Children are happy when their parents provide a peaceful and loving atmosphere…

When discussions are initiated about the love of God, the vast majority of conversation which is circulated identifies John 3:16 or the great love chapter, 1st Corinthians 13, as its basis. Certainly, we understand that God loved us so much that He gave His only begotten and, ideally, our love should be exemplified in the agape way of the Corinthian disclosure. Yet, I wonder if we give credence to the love expressed between the Heavenly Father and his only begotten, Jesus. Many religious scholars will try to disregard the relationship between the Father and Jesus as a divinely ordained prearranged relationship, but that's not the case. The relationship between Jesus and the Father was as genuine as it was divine. Jesus and the Father were absolutely inseparable, and Jesus reminded the world of his love over and over again.

John 8:28, 29 states:

"Then said Jesus unto them, when you have lifted up the son of man, then shall you know that I am he, and that I do nothing of myself; but as my Father hath taught me I speak these things. And he that sent me is with me; the Father hath not left me alone; for I do always those things that please him."

During Jesus' earthly ministry, He was never without the presence of the Father until he was crucified. Jesus reiterates this relationship in John 14:10 which states, "Believest thou not that I am in the Father and the Father in me? The words I speak unto you I speak not of myself; But the Father that dwelleth in me."

 You know by now that there are three major places in Jesus' life when he was *most* alone. The first was Jesus agonizing forty days in the wilderness where he primarily caused his flesh to surrender to the will of God. Next, was the garden of Gethsemane, where Jesus determined his soul to surrender to complete obedience to the will of God. The last major place that Jesus would encounter would be on the roughened slope of Golgotha hill. It was on the cross that Jesus was most alone. There was no multitude of crowds praising him or in awe of His glorious and supernatural miracles, no blood relatives to inspire, nor were there any of his disciples to help carry the weight of the world which now squarely and desolating rested on his shoulders. In fact, there were no angels ministering to Jesus, as they had during his transfiguration, no Lazarus, no woman caught in adultery, no Nicodemus or Zaccheus... the people Jesus gave his life to heal were not there.

As the blood trickled down his oxygen deprived skin, Jesus realized one more conspicuous absence...the presence of the Heavenly Father. I often tell fellow believers that I no longer know God as "God". Certainly he is God, but He is truly my Father. The most important relationship I have is that with my Heavenly Father. Until this point in Jesus' life, he had never addressed the Father as "God" nor had he even been separated from the presence of God. Yet now in the darkest hour on the darkest day of Jesus' life, His Father was gone. With a lifeless desperation, Jesus cried out to his Father, but now His God, "...why have you forsaken me?"

What Shall You Render

I dropped my cell phone in the floor of my car complete disbelief, as I tried to decipher the meaning of what was being said to me. As I checked my messages tears began to well up in the corner of my eyes as I tried to compose myself. My nanny has just left me the most painful message I had ever heard. "I had to rush Ericka to the hospital... something's wrong; she had to drag herself home from the bus stop." Ericka was standing at her bus stop when she suddenly felt an intense, hot burning sensation in her back. She was under attack and immediately was rushed to the hospital. The diagnosis was transverse myelitis. Transverse Myelitis is a rare neurological disorder, which attacks a person's spinal cord, and in Ericka's case left her completely paralyzed from the waist down.

It was at this point when I cried out to the Lord. "Father, what do you want me to do?" To this day, I will never forget the resounding and reassuring words that God spoke to me. "This an attack from the devil, and I'm going to handle this." The Lord then instructed me to the following words found in Psalms 116:7-12:

"Return unto thy rest, O my soul; for the Lord hath dealt bountifully with thee. For thou has dealt bountifully with thee. For thou has delivered my soul from death; mine eye from tears, and my feet from falling. I will walk before the Lord in the land of the living. I believed therefore I have spoken I was greatly afflicted: I said in my haste all men are liars. What shall I render unto God for all his benefits towards me."

The Father had spoken immediately about the ordeal – Ericka would walk again! I boldly marched into the hospital armed with the hope of God's word for Ericka. The devil wasn't going to win this one.

No one knows suffering like the sufferer. Those in the church who say suffering should be experienced with a stiff upper lip and a stoic existence don't know the reality of what it's like to hurt in a situation. The fact is it is okay to question God about why you're going through. I have never asked God a question in that He wouldn't answer. The principle truth of real suffering is that one never knows how they are going to react to the crisis at hand. Some may weep uncontrollably, a few may laugh involuntarily, and still others may pray silently. No one can speculate on what form suffering will take. The sense of anguish and helplessness I experienced didn't compare to the pain experienced by Ericka. As Ericka lay in the bed barely clinging to any hope of ambulation, her spirit remained high, but deep down I empathetically sensed her despair. I relayed to Ericka the words God had spoken, but they were words sent to me – these scriptures had to become a part of her new paralytic reality. As the father, there was nothing I could do; Ericka was the sufferer, this disease was Ericka's cross to bear. I have questioned Ericka about her feelings during the initial phase of her illness and she eloquently pointed out the following:

"At first, I believed the words you were saying, but then it was hard because it was like I was all alone. I was in so much pain at first. I was just standing at the bus stop when this sharp pain hit me in my back. Have you ever been stabbed? It was like being stabbed by one hundred knives at the same time. I felt like I was going to die."

Ericka Powell

But Ericka didn't die! The months following after her illness she began to undergo intensive therapy and, as of 2015, she has regained her mobility.

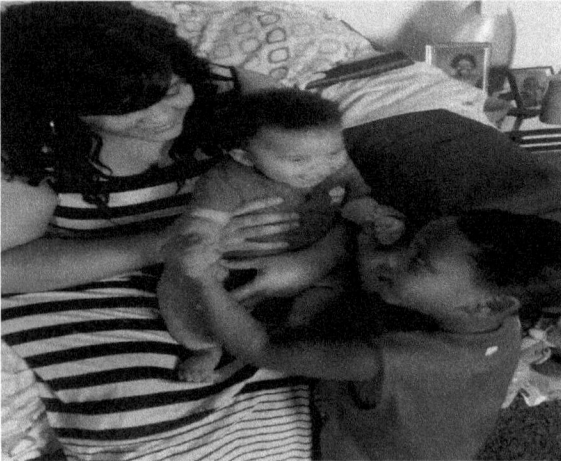

-Ericka Powell along with grandsons Elijah and Corey, 2015

Nonetheless the suffering Ericka endured was an ordeal that only God could deliver her from. I want to encourage those of you also suffering today, in whatever category you are suffering. You may be in a solitary prison cell facing life imprisonment or among dozens of downtrodden homeless people in a shelter. You may be being abused by your loved one with a sense of hopelessness about your situation, or in a stagnant, unproductive relationship. You may be a high level executive facing large financial hurdles or the poorest person you know. Whatever category of suffering fits you, I want you to know God has not forsaken nor has he forgotten you. Go ahead, question God about why you are suffering. Cry your tears, clench your fists, suck your teeth, and then get up from your ordeal! Some of you may feel like God hasn't heard you or won't answer you, but there's nothing you can ask God that He will not respond to in His way.

When Jesus asked God, "Why have you forsaken me?" it was a legitimate question with an even more legitimate answer. As a Father, I know that if there was something God could have done, he would have. But the fact was, He was bound by the Word he had already spoken concerning Jesus. He had already declared that Jesus was to be the sacrificial lamb for our sins. So as God saw His Son being hung on the cross, the Father deliberately withdrew himself from the earth between the sixth and the ninth hour. It sounds simplistic, but true – the Father left Jesus long enough for Jesus to finish the task set before Him. God also knew what He declared on the other side of Jesus suffering, the triumphant glory of his resurrection. You see, from a father's perspective I was only able to be valiant in my support of Ericka because of the word God spoke to me regarding her walking again. Without the Father speaking that awesome word to me, who knows how I would have reacted to her attack. What word has God spoken to you regarding your suffering situation? That's the word you stand on! If you can't answer what words God has spoken to you then you need to isolate yourself and listen for a clear, distinct answer for your suffering. Don't be concerned with what your situation looks or feels like, what other people say regarding situation or what attack from the devil you are facing. Stand, because on the other side of your suffering God has already declared glorious victory.

Romans 8:18: "For I reckon that the sufferings of this present time are not worthy to be compared with the glory which shall be revealed in us."

2 Corinthians 4:17: "For our light affliction, which is but for a moment, worketh for us a far more exceeding and eternal weight of glory."

Chapter 9

Marriage, The Call, The Walk

"The difficulty with marriage is that we fall in love with a personality but must live with a character."

Peter Devries

John 4:15-18 reads,

"The woman said to him, Sir give me this water so that I won't get thirsty and have to keep coming here to draw water." He told her "Go call your husband and come back." "I have no husband", she replied. Jesus said to here, "You are right when you say you have no husband. The fact is, you have had five husbands, and the man you have now is not your husband. What you have just said is quite true."

No one could tell me different. I knew that after previous relationships and failed experiences this marriage would be the one. After all, I knew her for twenty years and had always loved and respected her. After 11 years she came back into my life. Six weeks after reintroducing ourselves to each other after 11 years we did it...again.

There are many reasons why we get married, but, by and large people who marry do so in expectation that eternal bliss will be the result. Yet, our great disposable society has turned marriage from a holy institution into a rapidly vacated, very much maligned and naked structure. As I prepared this chapter and began researching various quotes, ninety-five percent of marital quotes illustrated sarcastic expressions about the benefits of marriage. People have lost hope in marriage. As I am writing this book I do so amidst an overwhelming tide of negative attitudes toward marriage. Great men and women of God universally revered are finding that their marriages are crumbling before their eyes with the eyes of the world curiously and judgmentally watching. What's wrong with God's holy institution? Is it the institution or the people in it?

Life in the army is in no way, shape or from a cake walk. The daily discipline doesn't go away regardless of how much you close your eyes and wish it would. On July 27, 2001 at the military entrance processing station in Baltimore, MD (commonly referred to as MEPs) I stood before an officer of the military and with my right hand pledged and affirmed that I would do everything in my power to uphold and defend the constitution of the United States of America "against all enemies, foreign and domestic." There was no leaving this commitment for the next 6 years regardless of any circumstance, the United States would hold me accountable to uphold my part of the oath. There are a very few exceptions that would allow someone to be released from their military obligation. Some are medical or behavioral, but ultimately, the expectation is that from the time you voluntarily enlisted in the military you will fulfill your obligation.

In understanding what has gone so drastically wrong with marriage, we can certainly draw several similarities between military service and marital life. There must first be an understanding prior to marriage that it won't always be so easy to be married. Marriage is a daily discipline that requires the same daily renewal that your relationship with God does. When you stood before God, the preacher, clerk of court, family, friends or whoever, you did so voluntarily (like the military). You said would be your spouse's mate forever and that you would do everything in your power to uphold your marriage. Ironically, most marriages have the same type of enemies, foreign and domestic. Foreign enemies to marriage are those third party issues which attack the marriage from the outside. External pressures such as infidelity and negative family influence are examples initiated from outside the borders of one's home. Financial issues, childrearing, sexual compatibility, trust and communication all contribute to domestic marital demise. Like the military, there is no leaving this commitment. You're in it for the long haul commitment for which you signed up- for life. There are very few excusable exceptions why you can leave this commitment, regardless of the circumstance.

Walking as one, living as two

The most powerful covenant that God has established in the earth between individuals is marriage. Peter Devries stated the following regarding marriage, "The bonds of matrimony are like any other bonds, they mature slowly."

Unfortunately, a great deal of marriages today contains individuals with little patience for allowing their relationship to mature slowly. Genesis 1:24 exhibits God's initial design for marriage. "Therefore shall a man leave his father and mother and shall cleave unto his wife: and they shall be one flesh".

You must understand that "one flesh" does not disclude the individuality in marriage. Although marriage allows you to walk as one flesh, you still will live as two individuals. I have encountered countless people who become so absorbed and wrapped up in their mate they lose track of who they are. God never intended for your mate to take His place, nor did God intend for you to lose track of the heavy call He placed on you. There is a flipside to this, though. Many times in marriages, couples become so absorbed in individuality, they cannot effectively interact and support their mate. God's design for marriage is that you walk as one flesh, but live as two distinct people in eternal marital monism. The simple definition for monism is two or more units that exist and function within a single unit. A dysfunctional relationship is far from healthy and disagreement is not sanctioned by God.

Amos 3:3 reminds us "Can two walk together except they be agreed." Many times there can be no unity in marriage because one or both persons have no agreement within themselves about the direction of their life. An individual who has internal disagreement cannot effectively fulfill the agreement of marriage until there is established clarity regarding the individual's personal unison. This type of person doesn't know who they are, can't decide on a career choice, has difficulty making decisions, doesn't know where they are headed or where they want to live....has no sense of settlement or completed self-development. This is what happens to many of us in marriage and is certainly what occurred to the Samaritan woman. Who is the Samaritan woman? In this chapter you will come to understand in one way or another we are all the Samaritan woman.

The Tools We Use

There are issues in your life that must be settled before you ever get married. The time of self-development for your life is critical and self-development is a never ending process. Throughout your life, you should have advanced enough in your individual life that when you get married both you and your spouse compliment- not complicate each other. The Achilles of a successful marriage is delayed individual self-development. You cannot possibly give another individual fulfillment if you are not fulfilled in yourself. Your appetite for contentment will never be curbed. Much like the Samaritan woman you will always attempt to quench your thirst with a behavior beverage that is temporarily refreshing yet permanently unfulfilling. People handle unfulfillment in different ways. Some people pursue a personal course of achievement by establishing worthwhile goals, and those receive the satisfaction others long for when those goals are achieved. Other people tend to pursue self-destructive behavior that leaves them on the brink of catastrophe. People who have chaotic lifestyles have such because unfulfillment and lack of self-achievement pulls them from the plan God has for them. Tools of temporary fulfillment *will kill you*. They will destroy everything God has planned for your life and before you know it you will be so far from God's plan and you won't know how to recover. There are many tools of temporary fulfillment. For some it may be the convenient craving of a crack pipe. For others it may be the seductive appeal of an alluring, adulteress relationship. Drugs, illicit and explicit sex and gluttony are just a few commonly used tools of temporary fulfillment that will cause you to stray far from the plan God has for you. The apostle Paul labeled these devices in 2 Corinthians 2:17. "Lest Satan should get an advantage over us: for we are not used by Satan to count you ignorant of his devices." For the Samaritan woman it was multiple marriages.

Let me tell you her story...

Her Greatest Shame

We know her as the people of her society knew her. We identify her as "the woman at the well", "the woman who had five husbands", or simply the Samaritan Woman. We know where she lived, but not how she lived.

Nameless, her story immediately conjures up judgments against her. She was asked the same questions you are asking now. How could she have had five husbands! Her choices in life left her hopeless, and she was ostracized by her society as nothing more than an object of scorn. Older women would walk away from her, rolling their eyes in disapproving disgust, children would mock her, and men would suggestively look at her with contempt, subtlety and disrespectfully hinting to be the next one. She had not planned her life to be this way. She was full of love and yearned to share it with someone who would sincerely return that love to her. She offered her all five times to be exact; in eternal covenant to men who left her. It doesn't matter why they left. Each time they did, she found herself alone again and wanting. Now, for the sake of convenience she decided maybe marriage wasn't for her; a temporary relationship might serve her better…at least he wouldn't leave her.

She had heard the great feats that God had accomplished for His people. When she was a child, her mother would rebuke her for asking the rabbi too many questions about God's miracles. She was used to seeing rejection. After all the entire Samaritan community was vilified by the Greater Jewish nation for being less than a Jew. At this point in her life she felt less than Jew, less than a wife, less than a woman. She had failed in her marriages and in life. She knew there was more to this life, but someone like her surely would never find out what the more was. Her best hope at fulfillment was now to keep him happy, so he wouldn't leave her like the others did.

She had overheard the men in the village talking about the Judean prophet who was rumored to be different than any of the other who had come. Dozens of men and women left their homes because the word was out that many miracles were being accomplished. There was even a rumor that this prophet had stopped a funeral and brought a young man back to life. (You know how rumors get started though, and, anyway, that happening way over there.) If He was the promised one, he would have no interest in a five time failure like her. She had already sealed her fate. Still though, could he be…

Anyway she thought, "Let me hurry up and finish cooking and cleaning before my man gets home. He's not happy when the house isn't ready".

She hurried to the community well to get some water to wash his feet as soon as he stepped through the doors of their house. She wanted to, for the sixth time, be the best woman she could be for her man. She would go the back way, because today she was in a hurry to please her man and she didn't feel like dealing with their scrutiny. Oh great. There's already someone at the well, now I'm going to be even more late."

The Sixth Hour of Your Life

There is something powerful about noon. There is no busier hour of the day. Noon is in the middle of the day, after you have started your daily tasks, but before you have completed them. Noon represents a time of change, a shifting from early morning preparation to latter day accomplishment. People can't wait for noon; because it's at noon we often refresh ourselves from early day vocation and have a few moments to exhale from the hustle and bustle of life. The Bible often refers to noonday at the sixth hour. There is often a sense of relief at noon from the already accomplished tasks, but anticipation of the coming tasks which lay ahead. It was at noon when Jesus began to be crucified. Noon represents transition and whenever the Bible speaks of noon something major is about to occur. It is here at noon or the sixth hour that Jesus met the Samaritan, and it is here at the sixth hour that God wants to meet you.

I like how the King James Version states Jesus passion for meeting the Samaritan Woman. "And he must needs to thru Samaria" (John 4:2).

Jesus didn't have to go through Samaria, he wanted to. The unfulfilled call on the Samaritan woman's life was so important that Jesus made a deliberate trip to deal with her failed life. Although society viewed her life over, Jesus declared that she was only at the sixth hour of her life. Many of you who are reading this book are much like the Samaritan woman. I have also used and failed with the temporary tool of multiple marriages.

I have come to declare to you that regardless of the temporary tool you have used to find fulfillment for your life, your life is only in the transition phase, or sixth hour of your life. You are so important to God that he will come right where you are. You know people may be familiar with your life, but that doesn't mean they know how you live. As with the Samaritan woman, society may have already passed judgment on you.

They may hypocritically judge you on your failures or even your prior choices. The truth is the mistakes you made are your mistakes and only Jesus has the power to judge you. Society will ostracize you for your mistakes, but while society is jeering you, God is cheering you on. Your mistakes may have cost you time, money and relationships and left you all alone, but God has still made a heavy call investment in your life. It's at these alone times that you are most vulnerable to settle. God doesn't want you to settle. He wants you to wait on the sixth hour, because change is about to come. You may see others and think less of yourself, but God does not. He just wants to meet you where you are.

The dialogue between Jesus and the Samaritan woman was exact, profound, and life changing. The first thing Jesus did was place a demand on her life. In verse 7 Jesus says, "Give me to drink". God has placed a demand for your life and wants to know how you are going to respond to the demand placed on you. God is not interested in why you think you can't fulfill His call. He only wants you to take the steps *to do* the assigned call. Regardless of the situation, you must first be honest with God about where you are at. I have a deep admiration for the Samaritan woman, because she shared with God here deepest shame. Can you share with God your deepest shame? Those areas no one knows about but God. As you courageously deal with truth about yourself, God will reveal more and more of Him to you and change what you think you know about Him to the actuality of who He is.

John 4:25, 26 "And upon this came his disciples, and marveled that he talked with woman: yet no man said, what seekest thou? or why talkest thou with her"

The more you come back to God and become intertwined in your relationship with God, the more people will question the sincerity of your walk with God. Not to worry, the same people who question your sincerity with God aren't generally sincere enough to go to God about themselves. They should be aware that every man will give an account for their own sin, so they should stop worrying about your sin.

The Kingdom's Gain

Vs. 27 """The woman saith unto him I know that Messiah cometh, which is called Christ: when he is come, he will tell us all things. Jesus saith unto her, I that speak unto thee am He."

She quickly pushed aside the hands of the man trying to help her. For the first time in a long time she didn't need the accompaniment of a man's touch. She quickly dusted herself off by brushing away dry dusty clay from the rocky pavement. The men who had gathered around her couldn't comprehend what had just occurred. There was a monotonous rumbling among them, but she barely noticed because her reddened and misty eyes were fixed on Him. She didn't mean to stumble, but the magnitude of His words had but for a moment caused her an unexpected moment of swaying, as she lost her balance under the escalating afternoon heat. She awkwardly backpedaled away from the small group. Her eyes were fixated with His- He knew her and now... she knew Him.

The presence that filled her was one of adoration, conviction, and love. He reached His hand out to her as if to welcome her to the love she had never experienced, but now felt. She grasped his hand with both of hers just long enough to return the love. Then with all of her strength she turned and sprinted back to open marketplace where the vendors and buyers had now gathered as a convoluted mass of hundreds.

It was three quarters of a mile to the marketplace, but, for the woman, each step was a fatal dagger to the hopelessness she had experienced for so long. After what seemed like an eternity, she reached the steps of the synagogue where the local rabbis and leading men often gathered. She paused for a few seconds, bending over to reclaim her breath. She then bravely pushed her way through the men gathered there. When she reached the top steps, she turned and faced the critical community that had so long ago ceased to welcome her. Still winded, she could barely muster the words that urgently wanted to leap from the deepest recesses of her soul. "He's here..." she almost inaudibly proclaimed. "What" the crowd replied. "What do you want?" The rabbi snappingly asked as he approached her. Suddenly in that instant a bold force surged from within her, and the woman we know as Samaritan once again became Abigail (fictional name), daughter of God. "He's here…The Messiah is here!"

Reclaim Your Name

It's not clear whether Abigail ever married again and truthfully that's not even the point. You may be wondering why I chose to give Abigail a fictitious name. The reason is because Abigail, like so many of us, lost her identity when she underwent the challenge of transition. You, like Abigail, have an identity. Even if the world doesn't know your name, God does and will do whatever is necessary to manifest the heavy call in your life. You also have a purpose assigned specifically to your name. If you don't know your divine identity, you don't know your divine purpose. Abigail's assignment was to proclaim the Messiah to the people of Samaria. She did in the face of those who ridiculed her. It was because Abigail was up front and honest about her mistakes that Jesus fully was able to reveal himself to her and she became a vessel of testimony for what Jesus did for here. Abigail found herself in the revelation of God's Word. Her new name became the Kingdom's gain. Many other Samaritans come to the saving knowledge of Christ because of her testimony.

Vs. 39 "And many of the Samaritans of that city believed on him for the saying of the woman".

The story of "Abigail" is often taken lightly. Christians pass over this story like society passed over Abigail. Yet it is one of the most powerful testimonies of God's compassion and willingness to do whatever it takes to lead away from the "water pots" of life. Like Abigail, you have endured the pain. Like Abigail you experienced the shame, like Abigail you must embrace the change. Like Abigail, you must reclaim your name. The e world's loss is the Kingdom's gain!

The key to your life and the success of your marriage, whether present or future is in understanding the richness of your powerful calling. Whether you are single or married let nothing keep you from surrendering everything in your being to God.

Chapter 10

Into Thy Hands

(The Final and Good Surrender)

We must come to conclusion. The conclusion of which I speak is not the finality of this book. Rather, it is the settling of the unfulfilled destiny of our lives. The destiny you choose is the call that you answer. Satan will call you to destruction, your unsanctified being will call you self-gratification, but God's heavy call will bring you to eternal rest in the Holy of Holies.

Luke 23:46:

"And it was about the sixth hour, and there was a darkness over all the earth until the ninth hour. And the sun was darkened and the veil was rent in the midst. And when Jesus had cried out with a loud voice, he said, "Father, into thy hands I commend my spirit." And having said this, he gave up the ghost

You Can't Quit

By my fourth week in basic training I became completely exasperated with the whole citizen to soldier process. I was not the most organized of individuals, and by this time I felt like I was falling behind the rest of my platoon in my organizational skills. I became ill my fourth day in basic training and I had to endure two weeks of physical therapy to recover from the illness. War was on the horizon and no one had anticipated it. The soldiers I entered basic training with were now gone and I didn't really know this new group of recruits. Every day was difficult in these first weeks. There had already been some voluntary and involuntary evictions from military service. Grown men were quitting under the drill sergeants pressure to perform on their level. Several of these either blatantly quit or did something so as to be quickly terminated from military service. It was during these first few days and weeks that I felt so alone...I am somewhat reluctant to admit that I wanted to quit, too.

-physical training at Fort Sill

It is in the most difficult of times you find out the most about yourself. Just as human beings have embedded within them a unique pattern of skills, values and talents, we also have varying levels of determination when it comes to facing the pressures of life. As a counselor to the mentally disabled, a pastor to the masses and someone who has simply gone through hell and back, I have witnessed countless number of people's reactions to the pressures of life. Some people are stern and resolute in their storm, while others absolutely lose their minds. I have noticed an alarmingly rising population of people who suffer from anxiety and anguish because they have difficulty coping with the cruelty life can present. Life can be cruel for sure, but it is in these times when you must decide if you are going to quit or keep fighting for yourself. Life, by design, can by far seem like an aberration of God's plan for your existence. God knows His plans for you, but you must know and, if you quit, *you will never know*.

Although my mind and at times my body wanted to quit the army, I found the strength to finish my training in these words. "He will hasten his word to perform it." (Jeremiah 1:12)

I began to ask God to hasten the days of training. Remember, there is nothing you can ask God that He will not answer for you. Based on this understanding, I asked God to speed up my time as a recruit. Almost immediately, it seemed as if the days began to hurriedly fly by. Before I knew it, I was standing on stage graduating from basic training as a full-fledged soldier in the United States Army…

Bad Surrender/ Good Surrender

In the Kingdom of God there are two types of surrender. There is that type of surrender which is bad – fruitless and then there is a type of surrender that is ordained by God and produces the best of you. Both are based in giving up yourself, but only one will allow you to live again. Surrendering, by definition means "to relinquish possession or control of to another because of demand or compulsion. To give up in favor of another." When someone mentions the word surrender to me, immediately connotations of the battle which produced the surrender immediately formulate in my mind. I am an avid war history buff. In my personal possession I have a collection of war movies. There is no intrigue for me in the sensationalized and glamorized violence contained in these movies. The interest for me lies in the behind the scenes strategy between two or more opposing forces for the right to call one the victor. Each side when possible extends overwhelming and fatal force to the other, until one party is placed in an inferior position of surrender. When one side surrenders, the terms of surrender are at the discretion of the victor, and the loser must submit or be subject to further infliction of damage from the victor.

It amazes me how many Christians don't realize the intense war we are engaged in. One side is the devil and his demonic forces doing everything he can do to cause death and destruction for any human he can. John 10:10 declares, "The thief cometh not, but for to steal, kill, and destroy." He can't war directly with God, because he has already been defeated by Jesus.

1 John 3:20 explains, "…For this purpose the Son of God was manifested, that he might destroy the works of the devil."

Therefore each human being becomes the devil's target. His strategy is to disrupt your life in any way possible. Notice, I said this applies to each human. People who are not Christians are still subject to Satan's attacks, but Christians are Satan's primary overthrow objective. You see, Christians have access to the divine weapons capable of hurting Satan's kingdoms. Think about it in this manner. An ISIS terrorist indiscriminately desires to kill whatever American he can. It doesn't matter what age, size, shape, race, gender the American, all Americans are targets of the terrorist's strategy of destruction. The death of American civilians in the twisted rubble of an exploding World Trade Center or Pentagon is not as significant to a murdering terrorist as the death of an American soldier, because the terrorist realizes the American soldier has the training, weaponry and ability to severely retaliate against the terrorist. Each Christian has access to the materials necessary to inflict serious damage to the devil. There have been times in American history when defeat looked imminent, but the American soldier has never lost a war. Throughout history, when an American soldier shows up for a conflict, the tide of the entire conflict changes. The same holds true for the Christian. There may be darkness all around, but when a Christian uses the weaponry given to him, the battle just became the victory.

There are many of you reading this book who are in the middle of a serious conflict with the devil. Your heavy call has placed a bull's eye on your life from the enemy and every time you turn around you are faced with challenge after challenge. Some of you even want to throw up your hands and say "I quit", much like I did during my army training. This is what I call bad surrender. I have a question for you...

In the middle of a war, who are you going to surrender to?

Bad surrender is when you cave in to the pressures of the battle in which you are engaged. The enemy will not blatantly come before you and tell you to quit. It always starts with suggestion in your mind. Although it starts in your mind, when you have a bad surrender, it ends with a broken spirit. The greatest example of bad surrender occurs in the book of Genesis.

Genesis 2:16, 17:

"And the Lord God took the man and put him into the garden to dress it and keep it. And the Lord commanded the man, saying of every tree of the garden thou mayest freely eat: thou shalt not eat of it: for in the day that thou eatest thereof thou shalt surely die.")

And the woman saw that the tree was good for food and that it was pleasant to the eye, and a tree to be desired to make one wise, she took of the fruit thereof and did eat, and gave also unto her husband with her, and he did eat."

Adam and Eve's decision to yield to satanic suggestion was really a case of bad surrender. It started with the devil's suggestion to Eve and ended up with spiritual repercussions for man that would not be removed until the Day of Atonement. Bad surrender will always result in separation from God. By relinquishing the promise God established for them, Adam and Eve alienated themselves from the precious presence of God. That's not the lonely walk God has planned for your life. From this point on in your life, this must not be the surrender you choose.

Be mindful that you will always have victory in God, but only when you choose good surrender for your life.

Up until this point, we have discussed two of the three types of surrender in your life. The first surrender is defined as the habitation of initial surrender and deals with the physical part of you. Next is the second, or soul surrender, which correlates to the surrender of your soul to the obedience and complete will of God. The final surrender for your life is what I call good surrender, the surrender of your spirit to God. Most Christians are under the false presumption that there is nothing in your spirit that you need to surrender to God. The Bible contradicts this theory, though. Everything that wounds your body or sabotages your soul affects your spirit. I have heard preachers teach for years about the living sacrifice of presenting your body, or the saving of one's soul. Both are true and absolutely vital.

However, the most dangerous attack to you is that which crushes the fabric of your spirit. Proverbs 18:14 reminds us, "The spirit of a man will sustain his infirmity, but a wounded spirit who can bear?" When someone's spirit is damaged it's almost impossible to get that person to function in any other phase of their life. The person with a damaged spirit must completely surrender those stinging, piercing arrows of life which caused the damage to the person's spirit. The final surrender is the most difficult surrender because it is by far the hardest to diagnose. When a person is sick the manifestation of the illness is usually more easily recognizable. If an individual has an emotional breakdown, well trained counselors are capable of quickly picking up the problem. A damaged spirit is not visible to the naked eye, nor is it able to be diagnosed by a single assessment. A damaged spirit can only be diagnosed by the Spirit of God. Therein lays the correlating cure. God wants very much to replace the damage that been caused to your spirit. Before He does so, you must first allow the Spirit of God to lead you in your good surrender. God has promised to restore your spirit and re-energize your life. As illustrated in Isaiah 57:15:

"For this is what the high and lofty one says – he who lives forever, whose name is holy: I live in a high and holy place, but also within him who is contrite and lowly in spirit, to revive the spirit of the lowly and revive the heart of the contrite."

Even if by self-caused errors you have caused yourself to be damaged, the mercy of God will speak to your surrender and heal your deepest spiritual hurts. Isaiah 57:18 makes this clear: "I was enraged by his sinful ways. I have seen his ways, but I will heal him; I will guide him and restore comfort to him."

Surrender, then Splendor

As Jesus hung on the cross in complete darkness, it appeared as if there was not hope for Him. As I stated previously, the sixth hour means change is about to take place. Often this change is formulated with darkness surrounding your life. As Jesus began to exit the world through his impending death, He did so while carrying all of the damage of our broken spirits with Him. Within the next and final three hours of earthly life, the bloodied scalp, nailed hands and feet, bludgeoned and pierced side would turn into splendor of the Holy and soon to be resurrected King of Kings. No one who stood by Jesus understood this magnificent transfer, nor did they understand that this was the final phase of His heavy call and lonely walk.

You see, you can't live again until you die. That is... until you surrender everything to God. A seed is alive, then it dies (germinates) to become alive again. You don't know what form it will become; form is determined by the one who raised it. We, as Christians, reap the splendor of the surrender we've sown. As Jesus surrendered His spirit to the Father, in a matter of moments he transitioned into the splendor and glory of the Almighty God.

Even while you are still in your darkness, God is calling. God is calling you to this good surrender. Even though it looks as though darkness will prevail over your life, if you simply and faithfully surrender, you soon receive splendor or fullness of God.

Conclusion

The Most Holy Place

Hebrews 9:9 "there remains, then a Sabbath rest for the people of God; for anyone who enters God's rest also rests from his own work, just as God did from His. Let us therefore enter that rest, so that no one will fall by following their example of disobedience."

Time to Enter In

"So take me in…to the Holy of Holies…enter in by the blood of the lamb." Excerpt from Juanita Bynum's album Morning Glory II: Behind the Veil.

There is a place in God's kingdom where there is no more struggle, only rest. You don't have to wait until you are transported to Heaven to get there either! It is the place where the fullness of God is experienced by you and you alone. No one can enter this place for you or with you. You are the high priest of your life, therefore you must be alone when you enter this place. It is a place of stripping and you must be there by yourself. I trust this book has been a blessing to you, and remember God would not have brought you this far on you lonely walk if he didn't want you to fulfill your heavy call. Let's close with a moment of scripture and prayer.

"And every priest standeth daily ministering and offering oftentimes the same sacrifices, which can never take away sins: But this man, after he had offered one sacrifice for sins forever, sat down on the right hand of God; From henceforth expecting till his enemies be made his footstool. For by one offering he hath perfected forever them that are sanctified. Whereof the Holy Ghost also is a witness to us: for after that he had said before, This the covenant that I will make with them after those days, saith the Lord, I will put my laws into their hearts, and in their minds will I write them; and their sins and iniquities will I remember no more. Now where remission of these is, there is no more offering for sin. Having therefore, brethren, boldness to enter into the holiest by the blood of Jesus, By a new and living way, which he hath consecrated for us, through the veil, that is to say, his flesh;" (Hebrews 10:11-20)

Say this simple prayer with me...

Father God,

I wholly accept the call on my life. I praise you for this mighty word from Your heart to mine. So many times I have allowed distractions to interfere with Your call on my life and my walk with You. You are glorious and as you are in the heavens, so am I in the earth.   Therefore, I ask that You remove every device, distraction, denial, disease, demand, or duty that kept me from filling my life with the magnificent splendor of your glory or finishing the course You have purposed for me. I surrender each part of my being to You body, soul and spirit in order that You would heal my brokenness. Thank You Lord for completing the work You have begun in me, and my expectation is stirred regarding my destiny in You. In Jesus Name, Amen...⏹

Bibliography/Works Cited

*All scripture references can found in the Hendrickson Parallel Bible. Hendrickson Publishers. September, 2005

Achtemeier, Paul. Harper's Bible Dictionary. HarperCollins Publishers Revised Edition. October, 1996

Bowker, John. The Complete Bible Handbook: An Illustrated Companion New York: DK Publishing, 2001.

Gove, Phillip B. Merriam Webster's Dictionary of Synonyms Merriam Webster Inc.

Powell, Ericka. Personal Interview. October 20, 2007

Quotes by Walter Bagehot, Pierre Charron, Peter Devries, Ralph Waldo Emerson, Epictetus and

Mark Twain are found in http://www.

brainyquote.com/

Soukhanov, Anne. Encarta World English Dictionary. Bloomsbury Press. 1999

The American Heritage® Dictionary of the English Language, 4th ed. Boston: Houghton Mifflin, 2000.

Fort Sill photos courtesy of sill-www.army.mil

TCU vs. Army pictures courtesy of Texas Christian University

For more information on this book or to schedule a book signing by Da'rain

Call : (904)250.1182 or (904)-993-9412

Notes_____

www.ingramcontent.com/pod-product-compliance
Lightning Source LLC
Chambersburg PA
CBHW031523040426
42445CB00009B/374